Mountain Biking In the Bay Area

Mountain Biking In the Bay Area

Volume Two, North from San Francisco

Michael Hodgson
&
Mark Lord

Western Tanager Press
Santa Cruz

Cover illustration by Jim M'Guinness
Cover design by Lynn Piquett
Maps by Phyllis Wright
Typography by TypaGraphix

ISBN: 0-934136-42-4

Library of Congress Card Catalog Number: 89-51391

Printed in the United States of America

Western Tanager Press
1111 Pacific Avenue
Santa Cruz, CA 95060

To our wives, Karen Samford and Sandy Lord, for enduring and understanding our need to write and ride. We are ceaselessly amazed, in debt, and in love with their desire to support and share in our dreams. For continuing to understand muddy floors, push our frustrated minds, soothe our sore muscles, and give up your time for ours we dedicate this second book to you.

Acknowledgements

This second book is the realization of a dream that both of us have shared over the years, the dream of being authors and writing about that which we love. However, this book would never have seen completion without the support and guidance of many wonderful people: park rangers, friends, and loved ones. We are very indebted to the following:

Sharee Eisinga and John Pannozo
Elliott and Hillary Dubreuil
Responsible Organized Mountain Pedalers of Campbell, CA.
Raleigh Bicycles
Jay and Shirley Supkoff
John and Ande Clapp
John and Debbie Emerson
Ranger Fred Lew
Ranger Wardell Noel
Bud and Norma Lord
Peter and Mary Hodgson
Tanner Girard
Doc Wanamaker
Doug Bender and Mindi Lord
Skeets, Concha, and Merritt Lord
Todd Vogel
Heidi Lord
Vicouna Hodgson
Shaws Lighweight Cyclery
The Folks at Catalyst Consulting
Bill Sunderland
The staff and rangers of the East Bay Regional Park District
Publisher Hal Morris
Editor Michael Gant
Publicist Lauren Wickizer

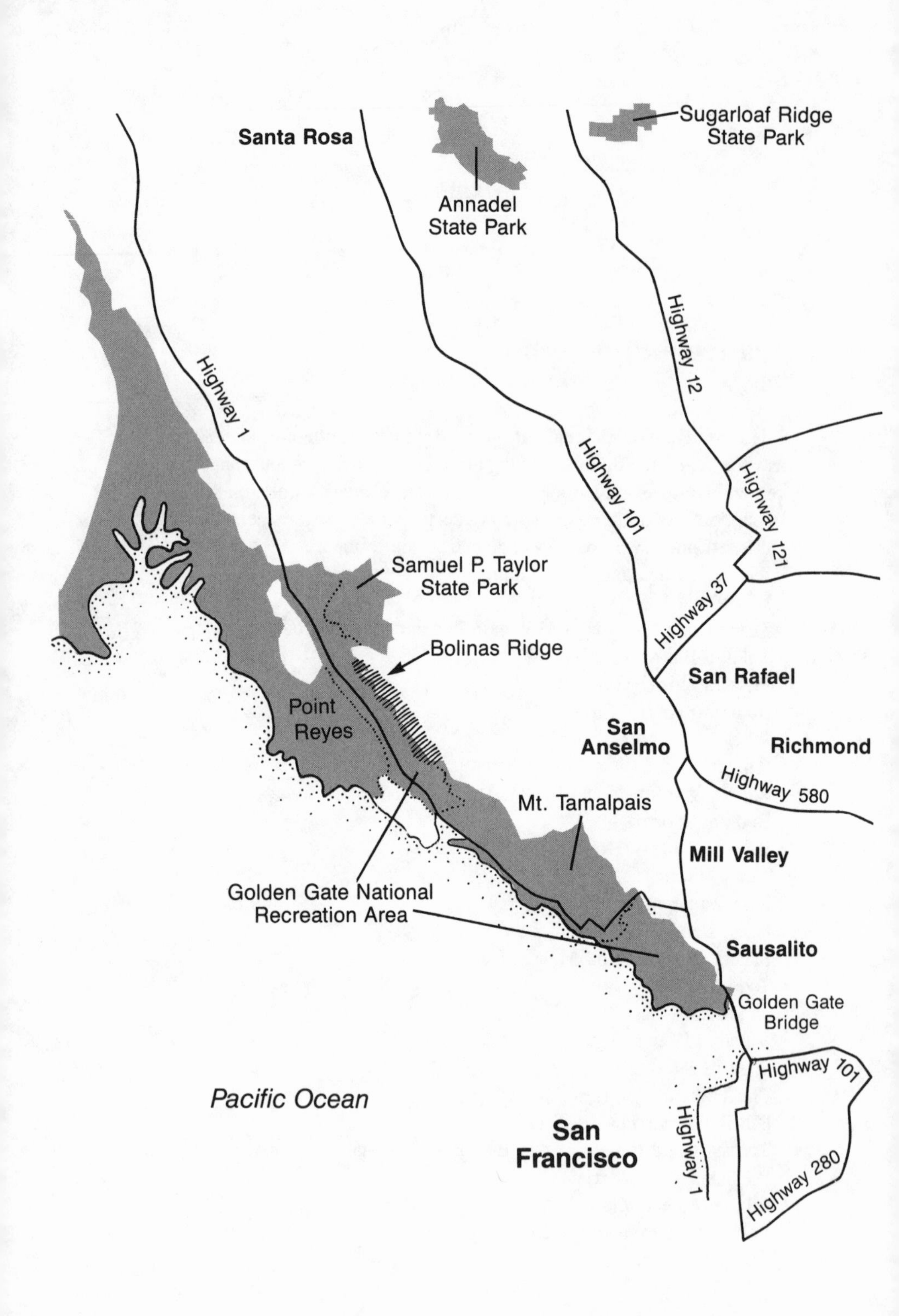

Santa Rosa
Annadel
State Park
Sugarloaf Ridge
State Park
Highway 1
Highway 101
Highway 12
Highway 121
Highway 37
Samuel P. Taylor
State Park
Bolinas Ridge
Point
Reyes
San Rafael
San
Anselmo
Richmond
Highway 580
Mt. Tamalpais
Mill Valley
Golden Gate National
Recreation Area
Sausalito
Golden Gate
Bridge
Highway 101
Pacific Ocean
San
Francisco
Highway 1
Highway 280

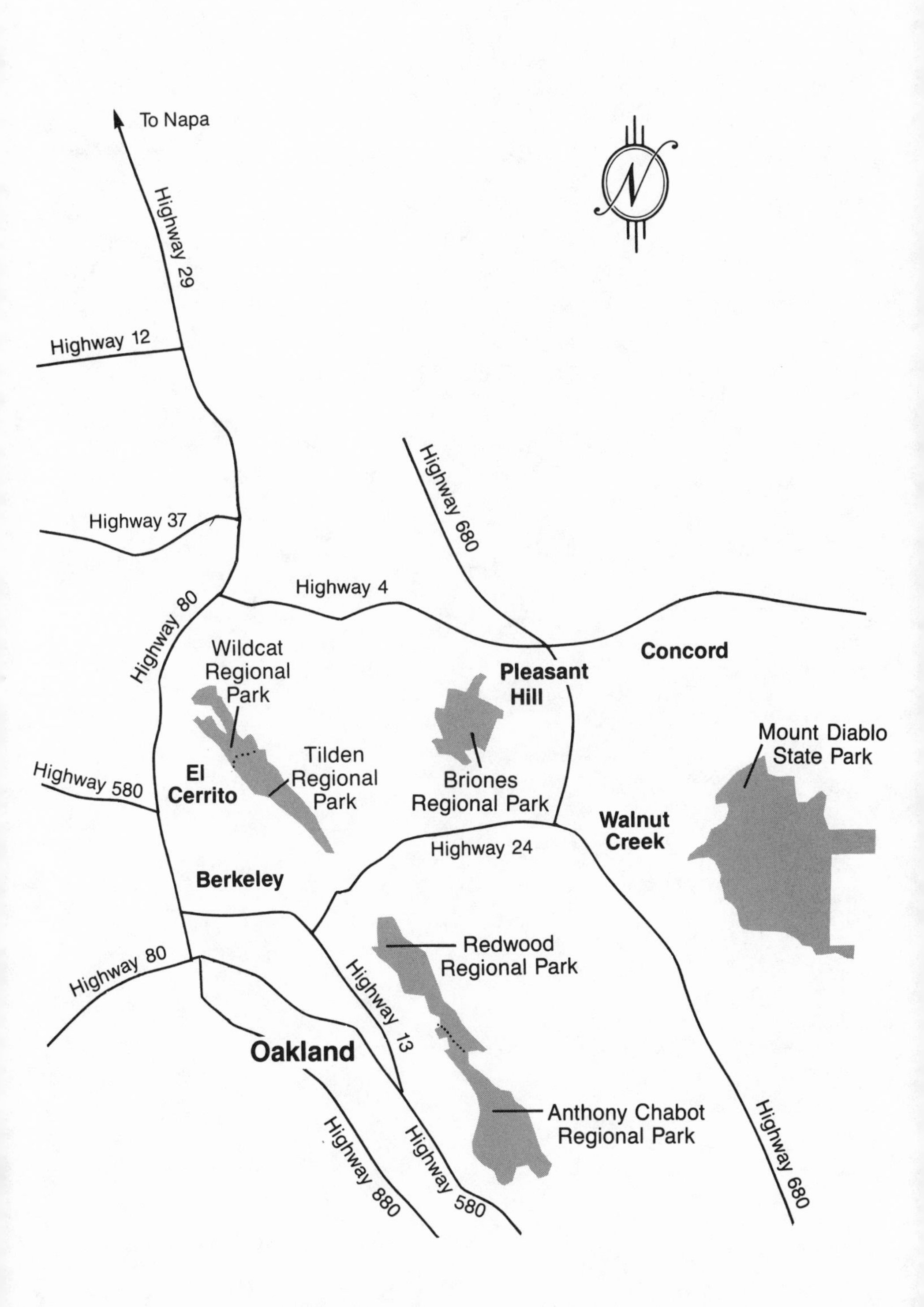

To Napa
Highway 29
Highway 12
Highway 37
Highway 680
Highway 4
Highway 80
Concord
Wildcat
Regional
Park
Pleasant
Hill
Mount Diablo
State Park
Tilden
Regional
Park
Highway 580
El
Cerrito
Briones
Regional Park
Walnut
Creek
Highway 24
Berkeley
Redwood
Regional Park
Highway 80
Highway 13
Oakland
Anthony Chabot
Regional Park
Highway 880
Highway 580
Highway 680

CONTENTS

Preface

Several years ago, just before beginning work on our first guide, *Mountain Biking in the Bay Area, Vol I: South From San Francisco,* I purchased my first mountain bike. Actually the bike is more correctly referred to as an all-terrain bike as it can go anywhere that I am willing to pedal it. Within days of my new purchase I drove to the East Bay Foothills and proceeded to attack every dirt road with reckless abandon.

With sweat pouring from my body, my legs aching, my head pounding, I dismounted (collapsed) and began to wonder what possessed me to buy a mountain bike. Suddenly, there in front of my sweat-burned eyes was my reason. A beautiful, tawny-colored bobcat was quietly watching me from not more than fifteen yards away.

The ten seconds that followed, until the bobcat faded into the trees, seemed like an eternity. It was then I realized that my mountain bike had become another excellent way for me to view the wilds. I still use my bike to achieve heart-pounding, gut-wrenching workouts, but I am ever more aware to find time to quietly coast and listen to the world around me. Because of my bike I have been able to view far more than I ever would have dreamed possible.

The dirt roads and jeep trails that crisscross the Bay area are the ''E Tickets'' to a backyard filled with more wonders than you've ever imagined. Take your time, ride safely, ride responsibly, have fun, and keep your eyes open. I hope you have as much fun ''discovering'' your backyard with this guide as I did researching (riding everywhere with a tape recorder and a grin pasted on my face) it for you. Happy Trails!

MICHAEL HODGSON

I recently took a close friend on her first mountain bike ride. It was a ''postcard perfect'' day, and we had spent the previous four hours riding without encountering a soul. It was difficult for either of us to believe we were only thirty minutes from a sprawling metropolis. As the day wound to a close we reluctantly dismounted our bikes and headed for home. Her ear-to-ear grin vividly brought to mind my first ride.

I had allowed myself to be coerced into a new trail "exploration" on a borrowed mountain bike. My friend excitedly explained that he knew of two fire roads and mumbled something about the vague possibility of connecting them. Several hours later, we returned happily exhausted, but without having discovered the mystery connection road. It didn't matter though, because we had experienced a world filled with wildlife and magnificent vistas that I never knew existed so close to home. We were euphoric looking back on a day spent basking in pristine meadows and "hooting" down spiraling dirt roads.

Those of us in the Bay Area are fortunate enough to be surrounded by open space, mountains, and a spectacular coast. You won't see 14,000-foot peaks or high alpine lakes, but you will find some of the finest coastal wilderness areas California has to offer. My hope in writing this guide is to responsibly present these incredibly beautiful and valuable areas that have been preserved for everyone to discover and cherish. Please help to ensure that others who follow will be able to do the same.

Ride safely, responsibly, and most importantly—enjoy!

MARK LORD

Introduction

Mountain biking is a sport generating much controversy. Understandably, a pedal-powered vehicle that goes virtually anywhere is enough to thrill the most adventurous of souls yet send shudders down the spine of many wilderness purists. It's not hard to imagine a hiker's anger at being startled out of a peaceful, contemplative state by an out-of-control mach-speed mountain biker. Yet, it is also not hard to imagine the joy of quietly pedaling along a ridge by way of a jeep trail bathed in early morning light.

A weekend visit to Mount Tamalpais is testament to the fact that too much publicity on one area can produce catastrophic results. There are hundreds of miles of fire roads in the Bay Area, many that seldom have more than a few visitors at one time. While we have no intention of exploiting coveted trails purposely kept "secret" by locals, we do wish to increase awareness of the vast wealth of mountain biking adventure to be had virtually outside our back door.

We hope to relieve the congestion of some areas and ensure continued mountain biking access in regions that are in need of public awareness. We have no interest in promoting growth in mountain biking in areas that are overcrowded, ecologically fragile, or political hotbeds of contention; nor do we condone their destruction. There is more than enough land for the hiker, equestrian, and mountain biker to coexist peacefully. Our purpose is to write a guide book that is responsible in its presentation.

The Bay Area is bordered by numerous open spaces, preserves, and regional and state parks; many of these areas are mountainous and blessed with a vastness that can make access difficult by foot. Frequently, a trailhead's immediate vicinity is crowded with hikers, although only a few miles distant the same trail is deserted. Mountain bikes provide a means to reach a destination in several hours that would take more than a day to reach on foot. An all-terrain bicycle, in the hands of a responsible user, becomes a legitimate tool for exploring the backwoods and foothills.

Perhaps we can help others to discover the beauty that exists just beyond our backdoor.

Despite the rumors and image projected by some, mountain biking is not just for the brave few willing to endure bone-jarring descents and breakneck speed. Mountain biking is to be enjoyed at any speed, even if you have to get off and walk for awhile. We've included rides that range from flat and easy to steep and strenuous. No matter what your mountain biking abilities, you may find yourself discovering wild places you never dreamed possible.

Mountain biking is as varied as those that partake in it. It is a dryland version of backcountry skiing or a quiet encounter with nature. It is a morning ride through a valley shrouded in mist or a zigzag descent to a river swimming hole. It is a social outing spent with family or friends or a personal experience with only you and the breeze in your ears. Whatever you desire, you will find something in mountain biking for you.

In the following pages, we will take you on a journey of the Bay Area mountains and foothills. We have tried very hard to give you a sampling of the joy of mountain biking in a variety of areas. Although every ride we describe in this guide was legal at the time of printing, it is possible that any trail could be closed to mountain bikes at any time. The park services may opt to close a trail because of overuse, erosion, or political pressure. Please, if any trail or road displays this sign , even if described in this guide, respect the ruling and don't do more to ruin the image of mountain biking by riding the trail.

It is our hope that you will experience much joy and discovery with our guide. However, this is just a starting point. There is so much more out there than we could or wanted to include. The rest is up to you.

Responsible Organized Mountain Pedalers Cyclists Code

The following is a list of "rules of conduct" for all mountain bikers to abide by. It is provided by R.O.M.P., Responsible Organized Mountain Pedalers of Campbell, California. For more information about this non-profit group, call 408-356-8230 or write P.O. Box 1723, Campbell, CA 95009-1723. "Thousands of miles of dirt trails have been closed to mountain bicycling because of the irresponsible riding habits of a few riders. Do your part to maintain trail access by observing the following rules."

Rules of the Trail

1. RIDE ON OPEN TRAILS ONLY: Respect trail and road closures (ask if not sure), avoid possible trespass on private land, obtain permits, and authorization as may be required. Federal and State Wilderness Areas are closed to cycling. Additional trails may be closed because of sensitive en-

vironmental concerns or conflicts with other users. Your riding example will determine what is closed to all cyclists.

2. LEAVE NO TRACE: Be sensitive to the dirt beneath you. You should not ride—even on open trails—under conditions where you will leave evidence of your passing, such as on certain soils shortly after a rain. Observe the different types of soils and trail construction and practice minimum impact cycling. This also means staying on the trail and not creating any new ones. Be sure to pack out at least as much as you pack into an area.

3. CONTROL YOUR BICYCLE: Inattention even for a second can cause disaster for yourself or others. Excessive speed maims and threatens people; there is no excuse for it.

4. ALWAYS YIELD TRAIL: Make known your approach well in advance. A friendly greeting (or bell) is considerate and works well; startling someone may cause loss of trail access. Show your respect when passing others by slowing to a walk or stopping all together. Anticipate that other trail users may be around corners or blind spots.

5. NEVER SPOOK ANIMALS: All animals are startled by an unannounced approach, a sudden movement, or a loud noise. This can be dangerous for you, others, and the animals. Give animals extra room and time to adjust to you. In passing, use special care and follow the directions of horseback riders (ask if uncertain). Running cattle and disturbing wild animals is a serious offence. Leave gates as you found them or as marked.

6. PLAN AHEAD: Know your equipment, your ability, and the area in which you are riding and prepare accordingly. Be self-sufficient at all times, keep your machine in good repair, carry necessary supplies for changes in the weather or other conditions. A well-executed trip is a satisfaction to you and not a burden or offence to others. Keep trails open by setting an example of responsible cycling for all mountain bicyclists.

In the photo above, Michael demonstrates the proper body position for downhill riding.

Basic Biking Technique

Although power, strength, and endurance have their place in mountain biking, finesse and balance are a good rider's main emphasis. Most difficult terrain and trail hazards are best maneuvered at steady speeds and in low gears. In all situations, concentrate on smooth transitions and shift gears aggressively. Anticipating upcoming gear changes is the key to successfully negotiating mountain biking's ups and downs.

Musicians and artists may speak of their instruments being extensions of themselves; the same is true for mountain bikers (think of yourself as the Casals of mountain biking). Visualizing your metallic steed as a tool instead of a bicycle might help you to think of it as an extension of your lower body. Proficient mountain bikers can negotiate some seemingly fantastic objects: fallen logs, boulders, deep streams, sometimes even all three at the same time (just kidding). They've ceased to think about what to do with their bikes and instead think of how to position their bodies. Very slight repositioning of hips or knees or transitioning weight from back to front or side can have remarkable (and sometimes unexpected) results.

UPHILL RIDING: For uphills, always start in the lowest gear; it is easier to shift up than down. Steeper hills increase the feeling of an unweighted front wheel. Compensate for this by slightly shifting weight forward. You must be careful not to unweight the rear wheel so much that you lose traction. A technique that works well on very steep hills is to rock your weight slightly back and forth; this prevents wheel slip and, most importantly, gives you something to think about other than how much you hate uphills.

DOWNHILL RIDING: Descending requires finesse and balance with the added element of control. Before beginning any significant descent, lower your center of gravity by lowering your seat post one to three inches. Shift the chain to the large front sprocket: this will prevent the chainwheel from engaging your leg should you become disengaged from the bike (only practical for extended downhill runs; rapid transitions from down to uphill require lower gearing and small sprockets). Pedals should be kept parallel to the ground with the front pedal riding slightly higher; this will prevent the pedals from catching the ground and causing an unplanned sprawl. While cornering, pedal weight should be shifted to the outside, forcing that pedal down and the inside pedal up; this will help you corner and prevents snagging your inside pedal while keeping your weight centered over the bike. Be mindful of keeping your weight on the pedals instead of the seat; it is easier to shift weight when necessary. Hug the seat with your thighs and keep your knees flexed and ready to absorb terrain differences. Injuries occur most often when excessive speed causes a loss of control. In the beginning, try only a few of these techniques each time you ride, lest you spend more time thinking about what you should be doing and less about the fun you're having. Relax, or you won't feel a thing.

WATER CROSSING: Controlled momentum and keeping your weight over the seat will mean the difference between negotiating the water trap or taking a swim. It is possible to pedal steadily through up to a foot of water by avoiding large rocks, deep silt, and bad Karma.

USING YOUR BRAKES: The key to successful braking, especially when descending, is using your head. Remember that the amount of braking efficiency is directly proportional to the amount of weight (your weight) that each tire is carrying. On downhills your front wheel is carrying a majority of your weight and even more weight is transferred to your front wheel when braking. Translated, this means that your front wheel (front brake) is your ''favorite pal'' during downhill runs and is more likely to control your descent without going into the dreaded ''locked-wheel, no-control skid.'' This is not to say forget your rear brake. Good riders learn to apply just as much brake pressure as is necessary for the terrain. Only practice will allow you to judge how much front and rear brake you need to provide control and avoid jackknifes, rear-wheel skids, and front-wheel lock up. Your body positioning is also important here. Ideal positioning pushes your fanny out over your rear wheel with your thighs gripping your seat. Experiment and discover what feels most comfortable to you. The more you shift your weight back over your rear wheel during downhills, the more you increase your rear wheel's braking power. Conversly, the more you shift your weight forward, the more you unweight your rear wheel and the greater the opportunity you have to demonstrate a swan dive over your handlebars ... not a pretty sight. The lesson here is to keep your weight as far back as possible. On level ground an equal use of front and rear brakes is appropriate because both of your wheels are equally weighted.

In summary then: the wheel with the most weight holds the greatest braking power; on downhills, shift your weight to the rear and learn to use firm pressure on your front brake with your rear brake as support;

never lock up your rear wheel on downhills.

TURNING AND DIRECTIONAL CONTROL: First tip, avoid oversteering at all costs. Second tip, relax. Many beginners and even experienced riders lock their arms and resort to the ''death grip'' while descending, especially when loose soil or ruts are involved. Learn to use your body and not your arms to determine direction. Keep a firm, but relaxed grip on your handlebars and initiate turns by slightly twisting your shoulders into them. As you twist your shoulders, your bike will follow (skiers will recognize this technique as similar to squaring their shoulders into the fall line).

MISCELLANEOUS RIDING TIPS: Tire pressure is an important ingredient to successful traction and ease of pedaling. We recommend, depending on the tire type, soft tires (between 25 and 40 psi, not mushy, but soft to the squeeze of thumb and forefingers) for sandy and loose terrain. For firm terrain and hard ground, again depending on the tire type, higher pressure is the norm (between 35 and 50 psi, resistant to squeezing between thumb and forefinger, but not rock-hard). Use caution when riding on soft tires as you are more likely to damage your rim and become the victim of pinched-tire flats.

Pedaling through deep sand is exhausting and technically difficult. This is one of those situations when your bike knows best. Relax and let the bike somewhat steer itself. Hold your momentum upon approach and entry. Downshift as low as is necessary without expending too much energy.

During downhill runs learn to ''bunny hop'' your front wheel over ruts, washouts, potholes, and other small unavoidable obstacles.

For energy conservation, use ''revolutionary pedaling,'' when possible. While pushing down with one pedal use your toe clips to pull up the other pedal. This offers you increased power and efficiency.

Keep your bike clean after rides. Accumulated dust and grit on the chain, cables, and gears encourages increased wear and tear and untimely equipment failure.

STRETCHING: The majority of biking injuries can be alleviated by stretching muscles before and after riding. Jumping onto your bike without a warm-up is very hard on your body, regardless of physical condition. Besides, a general five-to-ten-minute stretching program will also do wonders for your riding ability. Pay particularly close attention to stretching thigh and calf muscles; lower, middle, and upper back muscles; and neck muscles. Think of the minutes spent as insurance against months of recuperation caused by injury.

Cleaning Your Bike

Dirty, muddy, and/or sandy conditions will dictate that you clean your bike frequently—when especially gritty, after every ride. Grit and sand

act as a grinding agent, wearing down every moving part in your bike; the sooner you remove it, the longer the life of your bike and its various parts. Use the following as a guide to de-gritting your bike:
1. RINSE: Remove caked-on mud, gunk, and grime by gently spraying with a garden hose. Be careful of using high pressure as it is possible to blast water into the sealed bearings of the hubs and crank. Also, don't ever wipe dirt or mud from your bike with a rag; you risk scratching and ruining the finish.
2. DEGREASE: Remove the wheels and set them aside. Using a bucket of warm water and a mild detergent, scrub the derailleurs, chain, and chainrings with a bottle brush. Rinse, using the bottle brush again to scrub the chain, derailleurs, and chainring. You may need a small knife or screwdriver to help pry stubborn crud out of the chainwheel.
3. WASH: Using a floor-type bristle brush, warm water, and a mild detergent, gently wash the frame and wheels. A bottle brush is useful for getting behind the chainrings and other such hard-to-reach spots. Next, start at the hubs and work out, cleaning both wheels. Scrub the rim and tires with a floor brush to remove oil and tar residue.
4. FINAL RINSE: Reinstall the wheels and gently rinse off the entire bike. Once again, be careful not to blast water into the bearings.
5. DRY THOROUGHLY: Wipe off water with a soft towel. Put your bike in a warm place to dry. The tubes of your bike should have drain holes to help let the moisture out.

Lubrication

Now that your bike is dry, you will need to lubricate the parts that you degreased and any other areas that may need attention.
1. CHAIN, DERAILLEUR PULLEYS: For dry weather use a lube that will penetrate, such as Tri-Flow. Be careful not to overspray on the rims and always wipe away excess lubrication. For wet or muddy terrain, use a heavy oil like Campagnolo or Phil Wood. It does collect dirt, but the heavy oil displaces the mud and doesn't allow anything nasty to penetrate into your chain or derailleur.
2. CABLES: Some manufacturers recommend running the cables dry, but performance in very wet conditions can be improved with application of silicone to the cable end buttons and entrance points.
3. SEALED BEARINGS: Unless you are a mechanic, it is best to have your favorite bike shop do this for you periodically. It involves removing a seal, flushing out the old grease with solvent (like kerosene), drying thoroughly, and then repacking with new grease.
4. SEAT POST: Keep it clean and lightly greased with a heavy grease like Campagnolo.

5. SADDLE: Preserve the leather by rubbing with Brooks Proofhide and then lightly dusting with talc.
6. PUMP: Keep leather gaskets lubed with vaseline and rubber gaskets with K-Y jelly.

MULTI-PURPOSE TRAIL
YIELD
TO

Tour Format

For ease of use, each tour follows the same format. Pertinent information is presented first in capsule form. A full description follows. Before riding, become familiar with the tour by reading the trail description; this will lessen the chances of missing an important turn or, worse, spending the day with your eyes on the guide instead of enjoying your surroundings.

TOPO: This refers to the USGS topographic quadrangle by name and size; whenever possible, all maps are 7.5′ for best detail. These are usually available from backpacking or mountaineering shops. We are lucky to have a local USGS office in Menlo Park at 345 Middlefield Road, Menlo Park, 415-853-8300; they usually have the best stock. Although we include a map for all tours, these are only for rough orientation and are not a substitute for a topo map. Because of the long periods between USGS updates, trails are frequently not shown; look for major landmarks and cross reference with the included trail maps.

TRAILHEAD: For consistency, this is the starting area where the tour actually begins—not always where you have parked your car.

OVERALL DIFFICULTY: A comprehensive evaluation of the tour that accounts for distance, elevation loss and gain, and technical difficulty. Riding a tour in the opposite direction from that described will often greatly increase the difficulty.

TECHNICAL DIFFICULTY: Everything that makes a tour interesting! Includes severe ascents and descents, negotiating and/or avoiding stream crossings, sand, scree, rocks, boulders, ruts, water bars, gopher holes, fallen trees, and a few other suprises constructed by man or mother nature. The following are the gradations for overall and technical difficulty: easy, easy/moderate, moderate, moderate/strenuous, strenuous, and most strenuous.

A Note on Ratings: Accurately rating a mountain biking tour is very difficult. A myriad of variables involving weather, trail conditions, and temperature may drastically affect the difficulty of the ride; add differing abilities to this formula and complete accuracy in rating becomes nearly impossible (one person's leisurely cruise may be another's death ride from hell!). Therefore, use these rating as an overall comparison with other rides within the guide; if you've ridden a tour rated as moderate but experienced great difficulty, keep this in mind when selecting the next tour. Note that riding during times of wet weather will upgrade most rides one to two difficulty ratings—the easy ascent that we described may become epic in proportion; even flat rides can become nightmarish mud slogs (see "Rules of the Trail").

DISTANCE: The approximate total round-trip distance. It may seem obvious in the comfort of your home, but remember to allow enough time, energy, and daylight to finish a ride. Often the first half of a ride is much easier than the final half, particularly after gorging on a well-deserved picnic lunch. We have tried to be as accurate as possible using a bike-mounted odometer, map-measuring wheel, and official park mileage information. However, nothing is guaranteed to the foot.

HIGHLIGHTS: Relates the points of interest of an area, including the natural history, flora, and fauna. Although the Bay Area's recorded history is relatively recent, much of it is fascinating and colored by the entrepreneurs who were drawn to the area from around the world. Many of the rides pass through their realm; close your eyes and you may hear their ghosts still going about their business.

GETTING THERE: Provides directions for driving from major landmarks and/or freeways to the parking area.

THE RIDE: The detailed description of a tour. Usually noted are terrain transitions, intersections, stream crossings, forks, gates, and highlights of the trail. Although we have gone to great lengths to assure accuracy, we are not infallible and government policy on the use of mountain bikes is subject to change. Most areas described in this guide have a visitor's center. Inquire here about trail conditions and bicycle access; if this isn't available, look for an information board, which is usually near the trailhead. Remember that trails are closed for good reason—please abide by the rules.

TRAIL MAP: Outlines the trail description with parking, trailheads, mileage markers, and major landmarks. Maps are hand drawn from other published maps of varying scale and are only for general reference to aid in understanding the descriptions. For those exploring the more remote and advanced trails, we recommend using the trail maps in conjunction with USGS topographic maps. Some of the maps may cover more than one tour; each tour is noted with a number that corresponds to the ride and an arrow showing the direction of travel.

ELEVATION GRAPH: Illustrates ascents and descents (perhaps too much so!) by showing the gradient as a graph. Mileage is shown horizontally; elevation in feet is illustrated vertically. Included are major landmarks that correspond with the trail map. Some long rides span several pages.

Chapter One

GOLDEN GATE NATIONAL RECREATION AREA

TRAILHEAD: *Miwok*
TOPO: *Point Bonita*
OVERALL DIFFICULTY: *Moderate*
TECHNICAL DIFFICULTY: *Easy/Moderate*
DISTANCE: *6.8 miles*

GGNRA—South

Highlights

The Golden Gate National Recreation Area is a massive expanse of land set aside to preserve some of San Francisco Bay's most spectacular natural landmarks. The area was dedicated in 1983 by Congress to the memory of San Franciscan Representative Philip Burton, a leader in conservation and park issues while in office. Regulated by the National Park Service, the park extends to both the north and south of the Golden Gate Bridge, although our rides only encompass the northern region.

The GGNRA tempts the visitor with a little of everything. Redwood forests, secluded beaches, rugged shorelines, inland lakes, tumbling streams, and grassy hilltops provide an awe-inspiring escape from the confines of the nearby city. Don't be surprised by the solitude you will find, or the crowds evident near the most accessible areas. If you begin early in the morning and are quiet, you will probably be afforded wondrous glimpses of wildlife such as deer, bobcats, numerous hawks, raccoons, and, in late fall and early spring, migrating whales.

A word of advice, bring several layers of clothing. Many of the ridges in the GGNRA are exposed and extremely windswept. Early morning fog

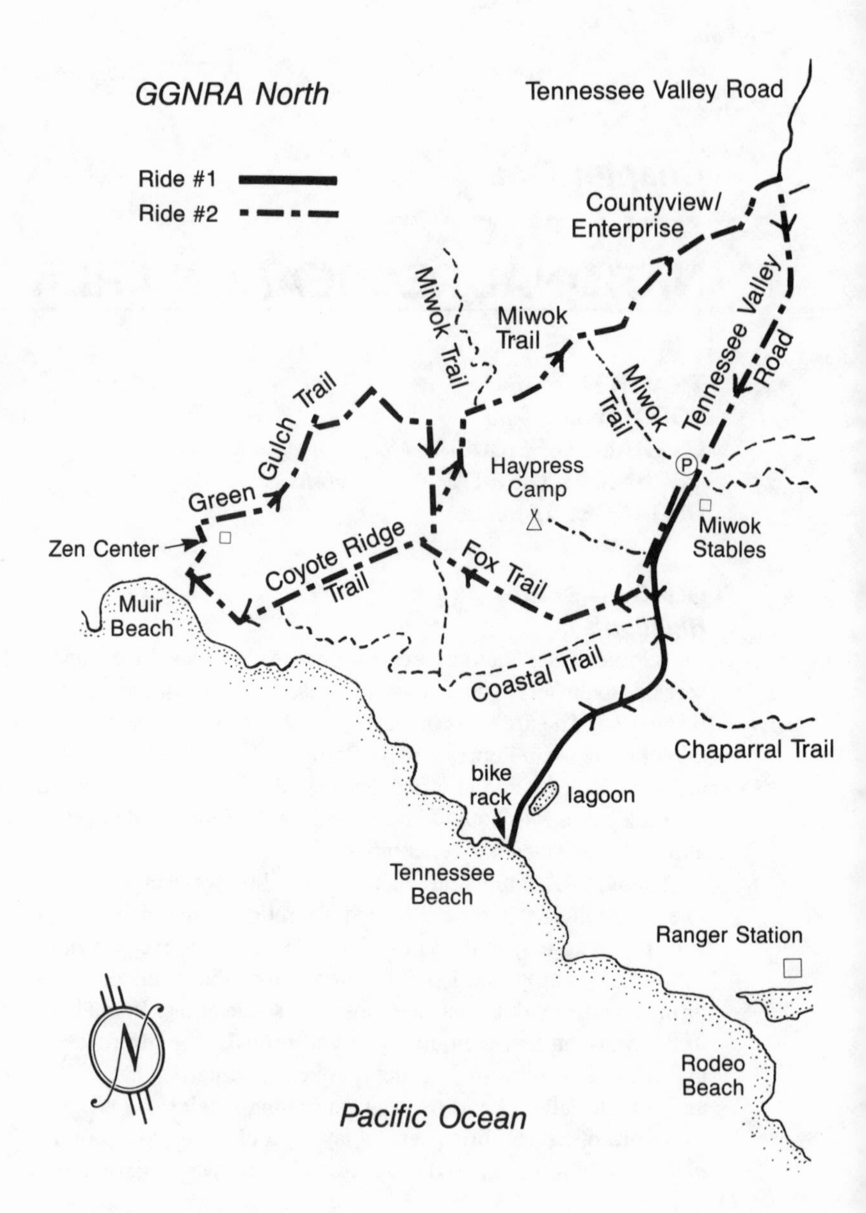
GGNRA North
Ride #1
Ride #2
Tennessee Valley Road
Countyview/
Enterprise
Miwok Trail
Miwok
Trail
Miwok
Trail
Tennessee Valley
Road
Green Gulch Trail
Haypress
Camp
Miwok
Stables
Zen Center
Coyote Ridge
Trail
Fox Trail
Muir
Beach
Coastal Trail
Chaparral Trail
bike
rack
lagoon
Tennessee
Beach
Ranger Station
Rodeo
Beach
Pacific Ocean

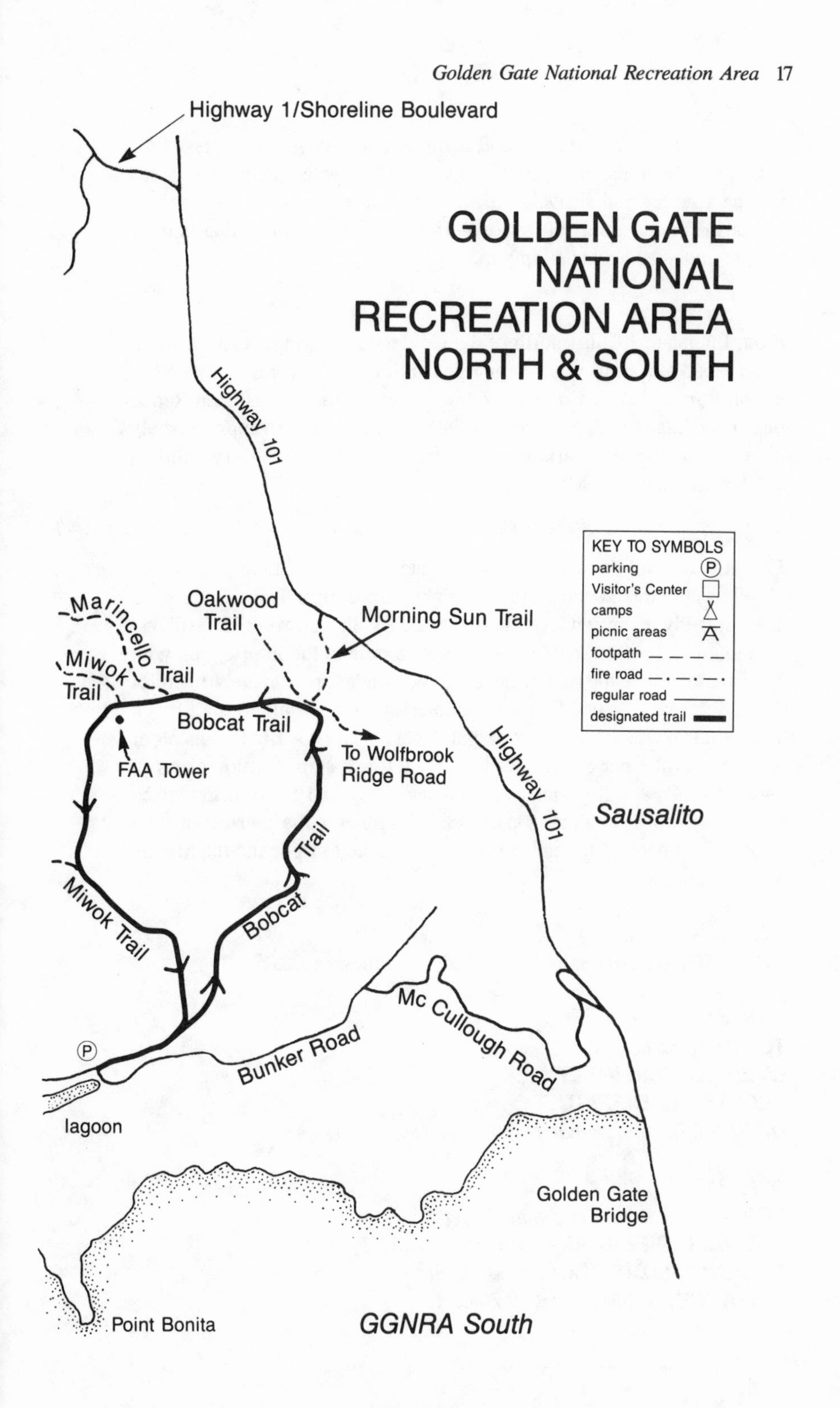
Highway 1/Shoreline Boulevard
GOLDEN GATE NATIONAL RECREATION AREA NORTH & SOUTH
Highway 101
KEY TO SYMBOLS
parking
Visitor's Center
camps
picnic areas
footpath
fire road
regular road
designated trail
Marincello Trail
Oakwood Trail
Morning Sun Trail
Miwok Trail
Bobcat Trail
FAA Tower
To Wolfbrook Ridge Road
Highway 101
Sausalito
Miwok Trail
Bobcat Trail
Mc Cullough Road
Bunker Road
lagoon
Golden Gate Bridge
Point Bonita
GGNRA South

can be quite dense, swirling, and damp and unless you are dressed for it can cut right to the bone; conversely, inland canyons can be solar ovens leaving you dry and shriveled like a raisin. Dress appropriately for all of Marin's moods and you will experience an environment that is truly unique and spectacular at anytime.

Getting There

From Interstate 101 just north of the Golden Gate Bridge, exit on Alexander Road and head west. Bear right on McCullough Road to another left on Bunker Road. Continue to the ranger station across from Rodeo Beach and Lagoon. There is parking here or you can return approximately .5 mile to a large dirt parking area in front of a large one-story building and the trailhead for Miwok Trail.

The Ride

The Miwok Trail begins just past the gate near the parking area. Pedal .4 mile to the intersection and bear right onto Bobcat Trail. Continue 2 miles steadily up until it levels and intersects with Oakwood Trail (illegal for mountain bikes). Stay left on Bobcat .8 mile to the intersection with Marincello Trail to the right (Marincello descends approximately 1.3 miles to the Tennessee Valley Road). Continue straight .3 mile to the Miwok Trail (south), which bears to the right. There is an FAA flight transmitter at the top of the peak here—well worth a lunch stop to enjoy views of Sausalito, Napa Valley, and San Francisco Bay and the San Francisco skyline. Miwok Trail winds and descends 1.4 miles to the intersection with Bobcat Trail bearing to the left; continue .4 mile to right and the Miwok Trail parking area.

GGNRA—North

TRAILHEAD: *Tennessee Valley Trail to Tennessee Beach*

Ride #1:

TOPO: *Point Bonita*
OVERALL DIFFICULTY: *Easy*
TECHNICAL DIFFICULTY: *Easy*
DISTANCE: *Approximately 3.8 miles round-trip*

Ride #2:

TOPO: *Point Bonita and San Rafael*
OVERALL DIFFICULTY: *Moderate/Difficult*
TECHNICAL DIFFICULTY: *Moderate*
DISTANCE: *Approximately 9.7 miles*

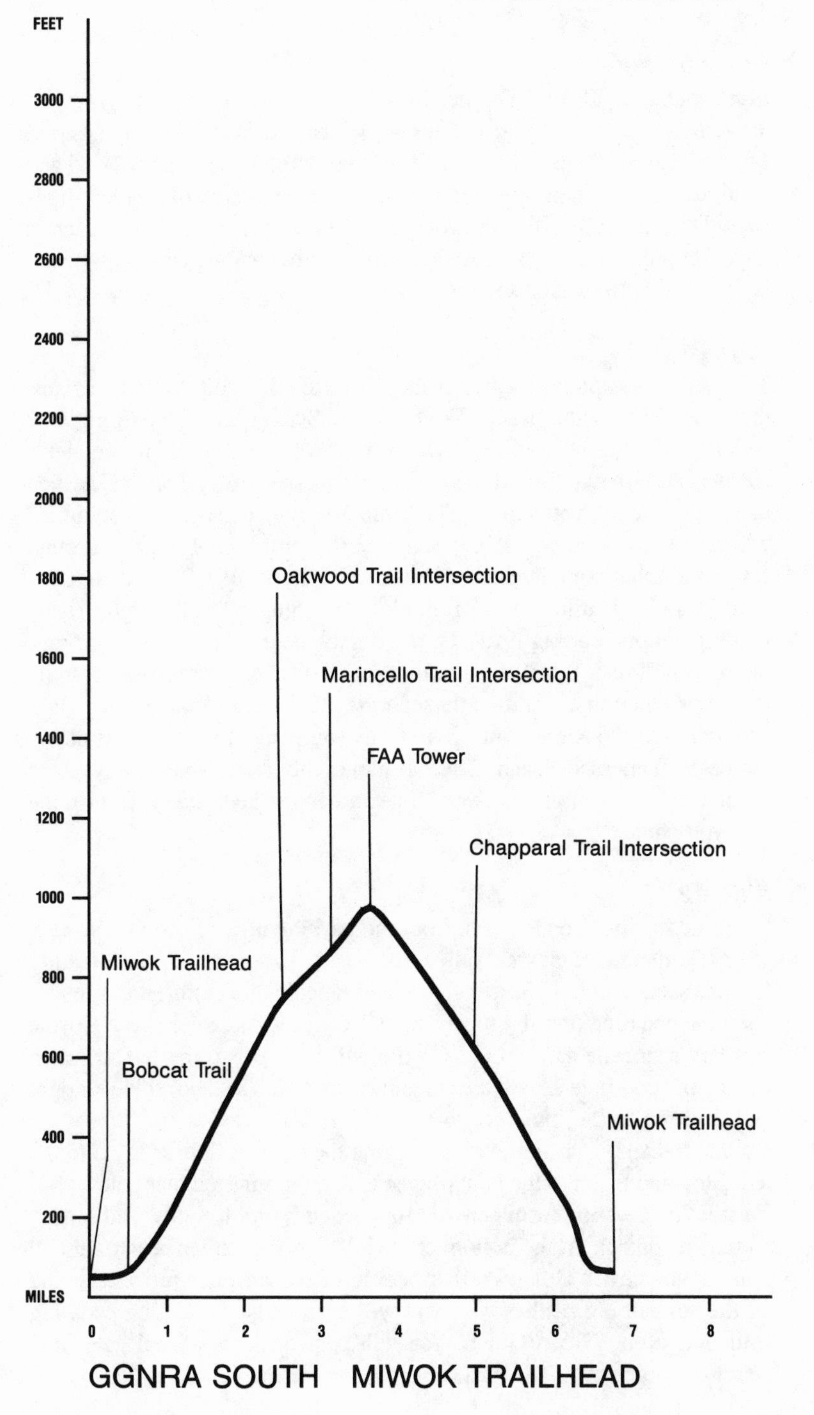

GGNRA SOUTH MIWOK TRAILHEAD

Getting There

From Interstate 101 north of the Golden Gate Bridge take the Highway 1/ Shoreline Avenue exit (north of Sausalito). Head north on Highway 1 toward Muir Beach (well worth a visit). Bear left on Tennessee Valley Road and continue until the dead end and the parking area by Miwok Stables. This parking area can be very crowded on weekends as Tennessee Beach is a very popular site to visit. Get an early start to beat the crowds—7 A.M. isn't as ridiculous as it sounds!

Ride #1

This is an outstanding beginner ride with little difficulty except perhaps the final hill near the beach. From Miwok Stables and the parking area pedal .3 mile to the trail to Haypress Camp branching off to the right. Haypress Camp is a .5-mile pedal off the Tennessee Valley Trail and nestled in a grove of eucalyptus trees. The camp is secluded and comes equipped with an outhouse, picnic tables, and several campsites. For campground reservations here or anywhere else in the GGNRA call 415-331-1540. Continue straight .1 mile to Fox Trail, also branching off to the right. (Ride #2 description heading up Fox Trail begins here.) Continuing straight, the road will turn from paved to hard-pack dirt. Approximately .5 mile from Fox you will cross the intersection with Coastal Trail bearing right and up to Coyote Ridge. Your road takes you straight and approximately 1 mile to Tennessee Beach. There is a bike rack here, so take advantage of the opportunity to secure your bike and enjoy the scenery. Return the way you came.

Ride #2

(Read description for Ride #1 from the parking area to the intersection of Fox Trail and Tennessee Valley Road.) Climb steadily up Fox Trail to the intersection with Coyote Ridge Trail branching left and right. You will continue pedaling uphill a short distance on a section where both Coyote and Fox share the same road. Coyote will head off to the left, through a gate, and continue across the ridgeline. Your path will continue straight and descend to the intersection with Coastal Trail. Coastal (illegal for mountain bikes) is a single track hugging the coast and forking off to the left. Stop and listen to the pounding surf several hundred feet below you. The loss in elevation from here to Muir Beach is rapid, rocky, and rutted, so stay in control. At the bottom of the hill, you can either bear right and join up with Green Gulch Trail or bear left for a view of Muir Beach and a little sunbathing. Either way, you will eventually want to be pedaling your bike along Green Gulch. You will pass through several gates and be on the property of the Zen Center Farm for the first .5 mile or so of

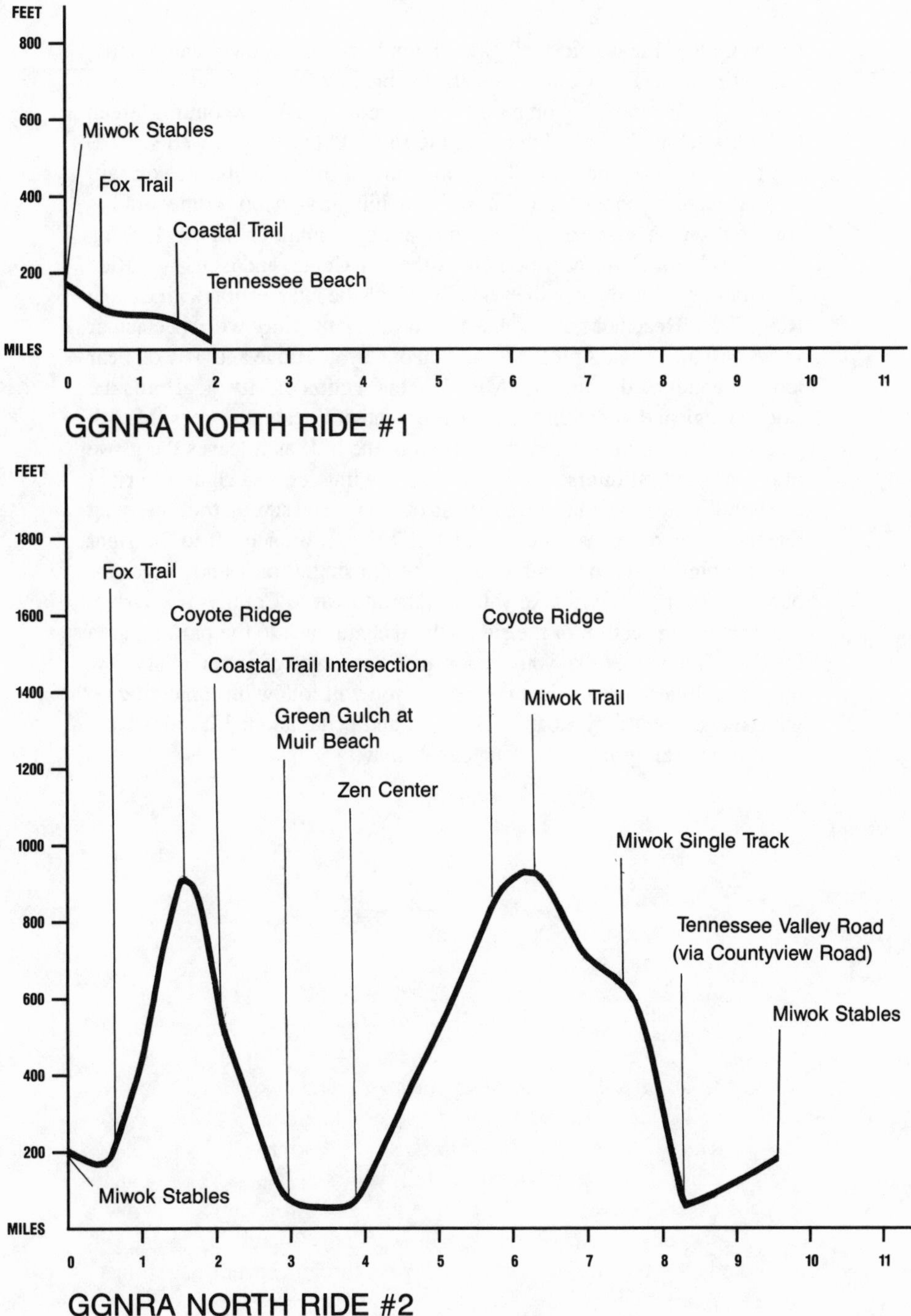
FEET
800
600
400
200
MILES
Miwok Stables
Fox Trail
Coastal Trail
Tennessee Beach
0
1
2
3
4
5
6
7
8
9
10
11
GGNRA NORTH RIDE #1
FEET
1800
1600
1400
1200
1000
800
600
400
200
MILES
Fox Trail
Coyote Ridge
Coastal Trail Intersection
Green Gulch at Muir Beach
Zen Center
Coyote Ridge
Miwok Trail
Miwok Single Track
Tennessee Valley Road (via Countyview Road)
Miwok Stables
Miwok Stables
0
1
2
3
4
5
6
7
8
9
10
11
GGNRA NORTH RIDE #2

Green Gulch. Please close all gates behind you, ride slowly and quietly, and respect the Zen Center's desire for privacy.

Once you begin riding on paved road, keep a careful eye out for Green Gulch switching back and uphill to the right. Everything is well signed, but the signs are small and easily missed. At the switchback, you will begin to experience the ''Zen'' of riding uphill through loose rutted trail—for what seems an eternity. You will pass by a small cabin overlooking the valley below. This cabin is kept by the Zen Center and is private. Ride slow and steady and you will eventually reach the intersection with Coyote Ridge Trail. Head left for a wonderful ride along the ridge with spectacular views east and west. At the intersection of Coyote Ridge and Miwok bear left and continue downhill on Miwok. This section of Miwok affords the rider a magical descent through a dense stand of Eucalyptus trees. Miwok gets somewhat confusing at the bottom of the hill, as it leaves the grove of trees. The first intersection is Miwok heading left and right. Go right and uphill away from Marin Drive to an open area and several trails merging together. Several trails, one of which is Miwok, branch off to the right and downhill to the parking area. These are single track and illegal for bicycles. Your path will take you straight and out to Countyview Drive. The remaining section of the ride will take you back to the parking area by road—remember that you are now in the presence of cars. Countyview turns into Enterprise Concourse, which you will follow until meeting up with Tennessee Valley Road. Turn right and pedal about 1.2 miles back up to the parking area and your car. Whew!

Chapter Two
MOUNT TAMALPAIS

Highlights

Officially designated a state park in 1931, Mount Tamalpais is the center attraction for one of the most visited and popular areas for mountain bikers. A potential mountain biker's paradise, Mount Tamalpais State Park encompasses over 6,000 acres with many fire roads that are legal and suitable for mountain bikes. In addition to this massive expanse of land, neighboring Marin Municipal Water District is the sole proprietor of the property surrounding Mount Tamalpais.

Yet all is not well with the mountain biking situation at Mount Tamalpais. The area is also a favorite stomping ground for numerous equestrians, hikers, wanderers, nature lovers, and others—and no wonder, the views and rugged natural history of the area are spectacular. Herein the lies the problem: Where do you draw the line and limit or control use of the park? The controversy continues to boil, causing some ridiculous and ugly encounters. While researching this book, we heard numerous reports of verbal and physical confrontations between mountain bikers, hikers, equestrians, and rangers that recall the range wars of the old West (sans Winchester rifles of course!).

Rangers in the Mount Tamalpais area have had to resort to setting up radar gun checkpoints and handing out hefty tickets to those mountain bikers exceeding 15 mph—not a hard speed to exceed by any stretch of the imagination. The Marin Municipal Water District is considering placing serious restrictions on the use of their roads and the closure of many others.

At the very root of these strict regulations is the problem of overuse and lack of communication and education at all levels—hikers, equestrians, mountain bikers, and law enforcement officers alike. At the time of going to press, no immediate or long-range solution seemed in place. Because of this we felt that it was in our reader's best interest, and the best interest of the area, not to describe rides in detail. We have included brief descriptions of some of the more popular rides for your benefit, since this is potentially a wonderful location to ride—however, there are other areas described in this book that we feel are just as memorable, less populated, and easily accessible for your riding pleasure.

If you wish a more detailed description of the Mount Tamalpais area, we recommend *The Marin Mountain Bike Guide* by Armor Todd, available in most Marin County bike shops.

Getting There

Located just north of the Golden Gate Bridge and east of Highway 101 and Marin. From Highway 101 take the Panoramic Highway/Highway 1 to The Mountain Home Inn. This is a very good central parking area for bike exploration. Farther along Highway 1 there is a ranger station at Pantoll, where they will have more information about trail accessibility and additional trailhead parking.

Railroad Grade

Set on the route of the once famous Mount Tamalpais Scenic Railway, Old Railroad Grade continues to be one of the most popular bike routes in the park. Beginning at W. Blithedale Road (just off Tiburon Boulevard) the route climbs steadily but gently approximately 7 miles to the top of Mount Tamalpais. Along the way you will encounter superb views; one of the most spectacular is from the veranda of West Point Inn, while sipping lemonade. West Point Inn is operated by a volunteer organization and serves coffee, tea, lemonade, and snacks for a small donation. There are even rooms upstairs for an overnight stay if you wish; check with the Inn at 415-388-9955 for reservation information.

Old Stage Road

A fairly easy connecting route from the Pantoll parking area to West Point Inn. Once used as a stagecoach route, the Old Stage Road provides beginners with an excellent opportunity to enjoy Mount Tamalpais. From West Point Inn, the Old Stage Road serves as an easy escape to the surrounding headlands and down to Muir Beach—remember though, whatever you descend you will have to climb later in the day.

Hoo-Koo-E-Koo

Named after the Indian tribe that once resided in the area, the route, though somewhat rocky, requires a certain amount of technical expertise. It is, however, an excellent traverse from Old Railroad Grade just above Double Bow Knot to the Marin Lakes area from on top of Blithedale Ridge.

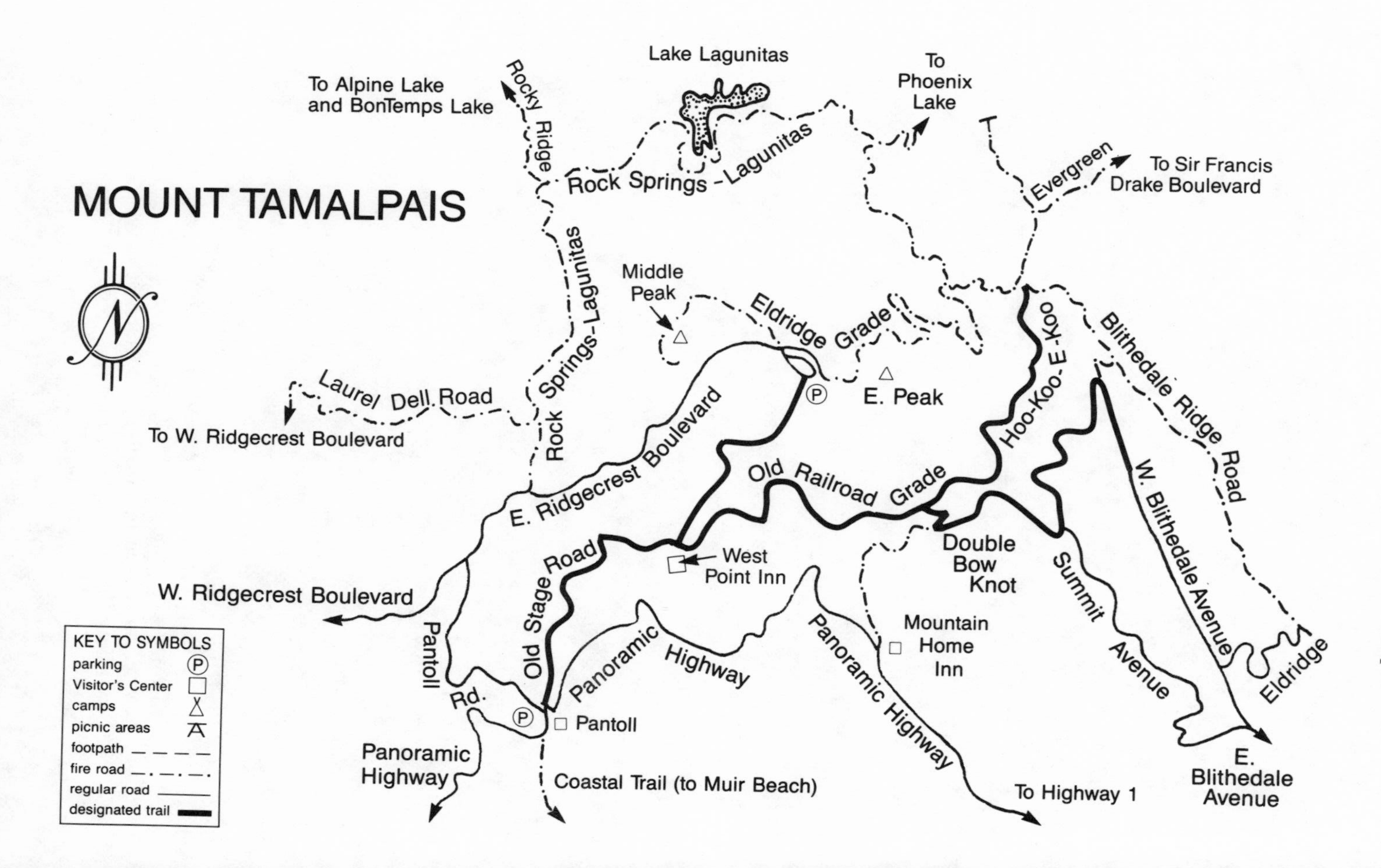
MOUNT TAMALPAIS
To Alpine Lake and BonTemps Lake
Rocky Ridge
Lake Lagunitas
Rock Springs - Lagunitas
To Phoenix Lake
Evergreen
To Sir Francis Drake Boulevard
Rock Springs-Lagunitas
Middle Peak
Eldridge Grade
E. Peak
Laurel Dell Road
To W. Ridgecrest Boulevard
E. Ridgecrest Boulevard
Old Railroad Grade
Hoo-Koo-E-Koo
Blithedale Ridge Road
W. Blithedale Avenue
West Point Inn
Double Bow Knot
W. Ridgecrest Boulevard
Old Stage Road
Summit Avenue
Mountain Home Inn
Pantoll Rd.
Panoramic Highway
Panoramic Highway
Eldridge
Pantoll
Panoramic Highway
Coastal Trail (to Muir Beach)
To Highway 1
E. Blithedale Avenue
KEY TO SYMBOLS
parking
Visitor's Center
camps
picnic areas
footpath
fire road
regular road
designated trail

Chapter Three

BOLINAS RIDGE

TRAILHEAD ONE-WAY WITH CAR SHUTTLE: *Bolinas Ridge, Bolinas-Fairfax Road*
TRAILHEAD ROUND-TRIP: *Bolinas Ridge, Sir Francis Drake Boulevard*
TOPO: *Inverness, San Geronimo, Bolinas*
SPECIAL RIDE INFORMATION: *Sometimes access is limited due to fire closure, therefore this ride is best enjoyed fall through spring. Call Marin Municipal Water District Ranger Station at 415-459-5267 for information.*
OVERALL DIFFICULTY: *One-Way—Moderate; Round-Trip—Strenuous*
TECHNICAL DIFFICULTY: *One-Way—Moderate; Round-Trip—Moderate*
DISTANCE: *Approx: 11.2 miles each way*

Highlights

This is perhaps the most varied and spectacular ride in Marin county. Bolinas Ridge offers the rider exalting downhills; a few gut-wrenching uphills (providing you are riding one way from Bolinas-Fairfax Road to Olema; otherwise the round-trip will offer the ultimate in 11.2 miles of thigh-burning uphill); mystical and deeply shadowed redwood groves; and incredible views east to Napa, south to Bolinas Bay, west to the hills of Point Reyes, and north to Tomales Bay. The road is hard-packed (provided it hasn't rained recently) and sometimes heavily used by equestrians, runners, hikers, and especially mountain bikers, so stay in control! There are also several cattle gates along the way; remember to close them and watch out for cattle when riding. Enjoy—we think you'll find that this is truly an outstanding ride.

Getting There

From Highway 101 at the Golden Gate Bridge, drive north to the Sir Francis Drake Boulevard (just south of 580) exit and head west.

One-Way Ride With Car Shuttle

From 101 take Sir Francis Drake Boulevard past Samuel P. Taylor State Park to a dirt parking area on the left side of the road approximately 1 mile before Olema and park one car here. The other vehicle will be parked at the trail head on Bolinas-Fairfax Road; from Sir Francis Drake Boulevard, turn left on Highway 1 at Olema. Drive approximately 9.5 miles to an unsigned left turn, just before Bolinas Lagoon and after Olema-Bolinas Road to the right. Climb a very windy 4.6 miles to the intersection and parking area for Bolinas Ridge Trail.

Round Trip Ride With No Car Shuttle

Park at either end. We recommend beginning at the parking area on Sir Francis Drake Boulevard, just east of Olema. Your ride will then be mostly uphill there and downhill for the return. If you wish to begin your ride from Bolinas Ridge Trailhead on Old Bolinas-Fairfax Road, see driving directions below.

On Sir Francis Drake Boulevard, pass through the towns of Kentfield, Ross, and San Anselmo to the town of Fairfax and turn left on Old Bolinas-Fairfax Road. Continue on this road, passing by Meadow Club Golf Course and Alpine Lake. The intersection and parking areas for Bolinas Ridge Trail are at the top of a winding grade, approximately 10.7 miles from Sir Francis Drake Boulevard.

The Ride

Pass through the gate and begin your ride at the Bolinas Ridge Trailhead on the north side of Bolinas-Fairfax Road. For the first 3.5 miles the trail follows rolling (some steep ascents) terrain through beautiful redwoods. At approximately 3.5 miles you will come to the intersection with McCurdy Trail branching off to the left. Continue straight, descending on the Bolinas Ridge Trail, picking your way carefully through exposed tree roots and ruts. Approximately 1.6 miles past McCurdy Trail is the Randall Trail branching off to the left. Continue straight and down, passing the cutoff to Shafter Bridge on the right. Near this point, the terrain opens into rolling grassland and the first of several cattle gates. Please be sure to secure all gates behind you. There is a rock outcropping at this first gate, an ideal spot for lunch and taking in the views of Point Reyes and Tomales Bay in the distance. From here descend to the intersection with Jewell Trail

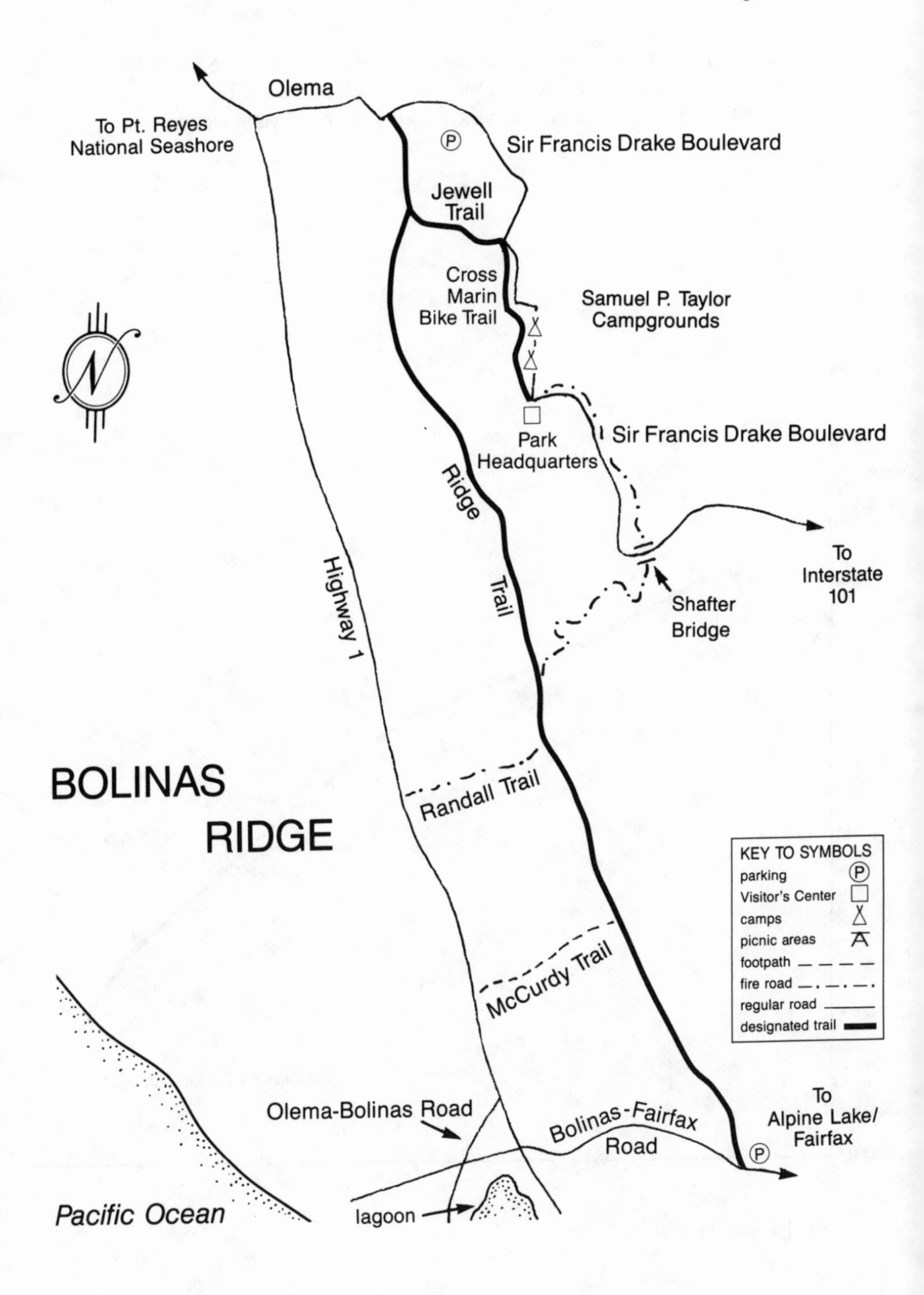

Olema
To Pt. Reyes
National Seashore
Sir Francis Drake Boulevard
Jewell
Trail
Cross
Marin
Bike Trail
Samuel P. Taylor
Campgrounds
Park
Headquarters
Sir Francis Drake Boulevard
Ridge
Trail
To
Interstate
101
Shafter
Bridge
Highway 1
BOLINAS
RIDGE
Randall Trail
McCurdy Trail
KEY TO SYMBOLS
parking
Visitor's Center
camps
picnic areas
footpath
fire road
regular road
designated trail
Olema-Bolinas Road
Bolinas-Fairfax
Road
To
Alpine Lake/
Fairfax
Pacific Ocean
lagoon

branching off to the right. (Jewell Trail will take you back to Samuel P. Taylor State Park if you are camping there). Bolinas Ridge Trail takes a sharp turn here and continues to the parking area and your second car.

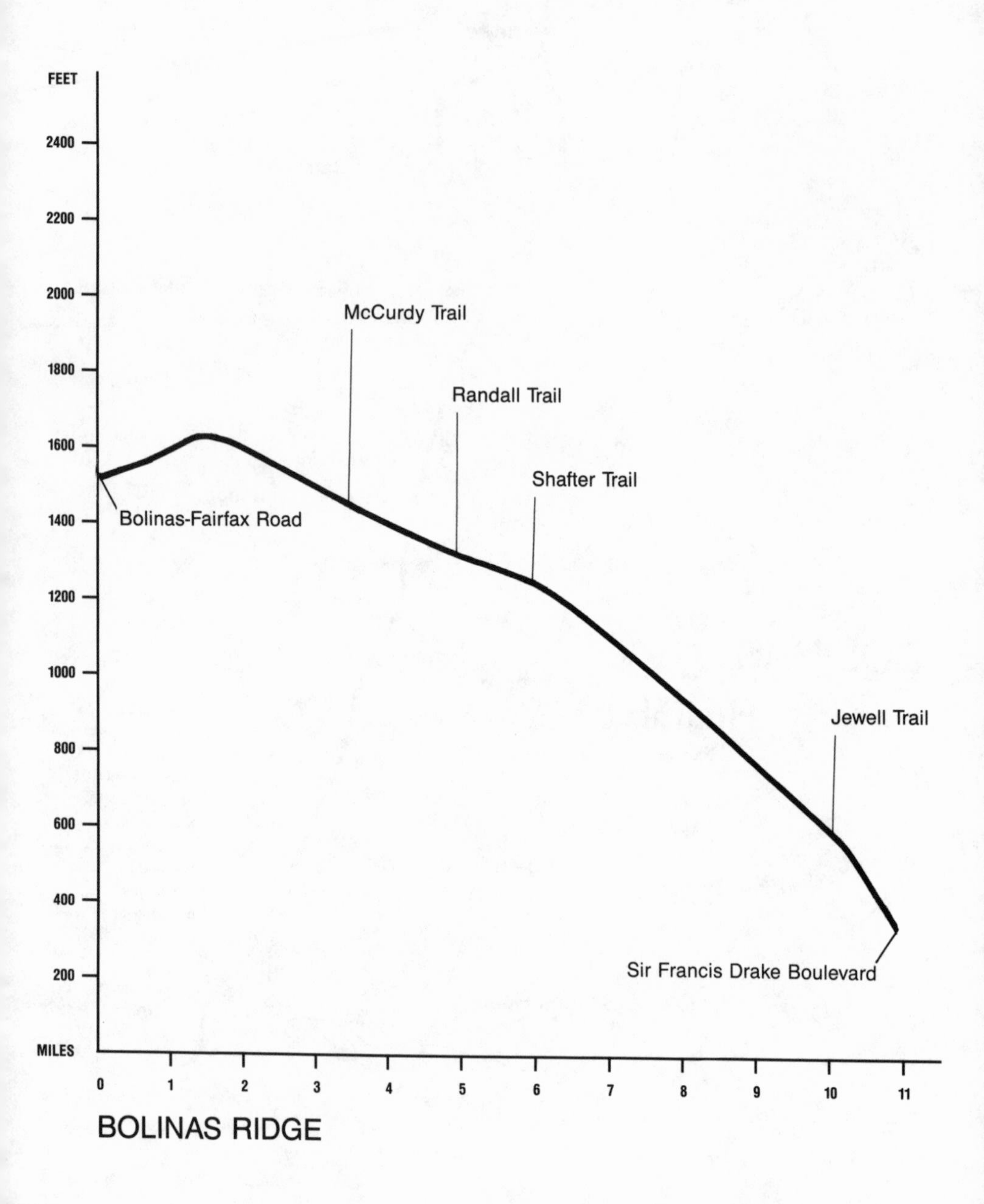

Chapter Four

SAMUEL P. TAYLOR STATE PARK

TRAILHEAD: *Samuel P. Taylor State Park Redwood Grove Picnic Area*
TOPO: *San Geronimo*

Ride #1
OVERALL DIFFICULTY: *Strenuous*
TECHNICAL DIFFICULTY: *Moderate*
DISTANCE: *Approximately 7 miles*

Ride #2
OVERALL DIFFICULTY: *Easy*
TECHNICAL DIFFICULTY: *Easy*
DISTANCE: *Approximately 6.4 miles*

Highlights

Located in the steep rolling hills of Marin County, Samuel P. Taylor State Park is an ideal base camp for experiencing some of the finest mountain biking in the north bay. The terrain varies from shady, cool creek beds canopied by towering redwoods to dry and open ridge tops with sweeping views of Tomales Bay and Point Reyes. We recommend exploring for at least a day or two if you wish to truly experience the area's treasures. This will give you ample opportunity to spend some time on Barnabe Peak admiring the inspiring view to the coast or to take a refreshing dip and bask on a rock at one of Papermill Creek's swimming holes.

In the late 1870s, the park's namesake once operated a paper mill (hence the name Papermill Creek) that supplied San Francisco with material for its daily paper; he also dallied in the manufacture of blasting powder until

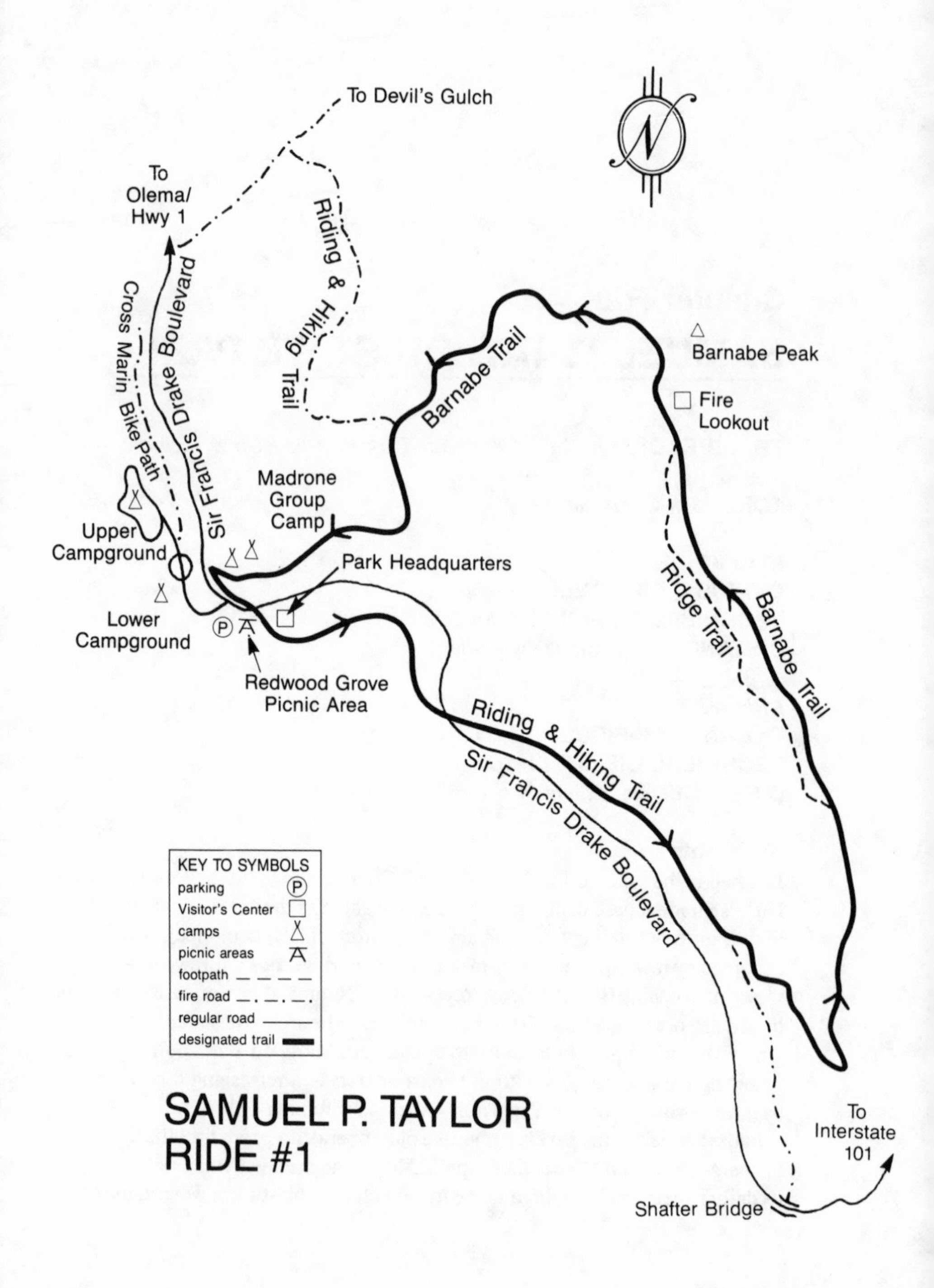

SAMUEL P. TAYLOR RIDE #1

SAMUEL P. TAYLOR STATE PARK
RIDE #2

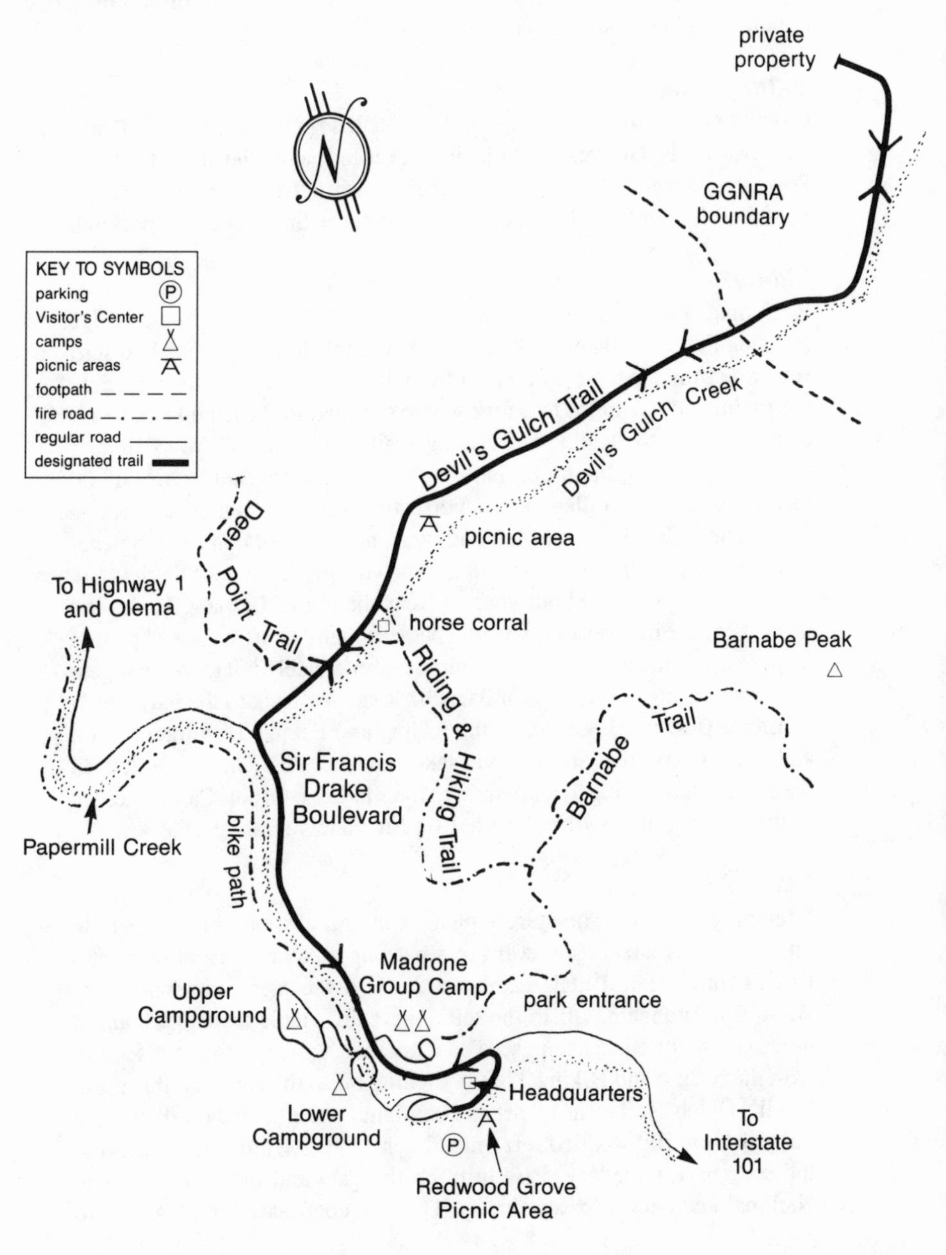

a rather explosive mishap brought this business venture to a close. Taylor later opened a camp and resort hotel beside the newly built narrow-gauge railroad; this was one of the first areas in the United States to offer camping as an outdoor recreation and became one of northern California's most popular weekend play areas.

Getting There

From Interstate 101 north of the Golden Gate Bridge take the Francis Drake Boulevard exit. Go west on Francis Drake, following the signs for Point Reyes and Samuel P. Taylor State Park. Turn left into the entrance for Samuel P. Taylor State Park and leave your car in the picnic area parking.

Ride #1

Beginning at the Redwood Grove picnic area, pedal .9 mile to the bridge crossing Francis Drake (parking is also available here if you wish to start your ride from the highway and not from the state park). Continue straight approximately 1.7 miles to a fork where the road to Barnabe Peak heads up and left and the Riding and Hiking Trail heads straight. You will bear left and up, and up, and up, and up—climbing from 200 to over 1,000 feet in just under 2 miles to the intersection with the single-track Ridge Trail. The Ridge Trail goes left and west, but you will continue to pedal straight and up some more—though somewhat gradually (our thighs were burning by now, how about yours?) Near the top of Barnabe Peak, and in sight of the Fire Lookout, you will pass through a short section of private land. Respect the privacy and exit almost immediately left at the first gate for a rip-roaring descent down Barnabe Road and back to the park headquarters. Descend 1.3 miles to the Riding and Hiking Trail intersection and a sharp left turn. Straight will take you to Devil's Gulch. Go left on the Riding and Hiking Trail .8 mile to the Madrone Group Camp. Return to the parking area by heading left on Sir Fancis Drake Boulevard.

Ride #2

Beginning at the Redwood Grove picnic area, pedal approximately .8 mile on Sir Francis Drake Boulevard to a parking area and a right turn onto Devil's Gulch Trail. Pedal steadily up .2 mile to the intersection with Deer Point Trail branching off to the left. There are picnic tables here and a horse corral for equestrian use. Pedal another .1 mile to the intersection with the Riding and Hiking Trail branching off to the right. At this point Devil's Gulch Trail turns to dirt and continues straight up the valley. Ride through beautiful wooded terrain and gently up 1.1 miles to a gate and the state park boundary. Pass through the gate and onto Golden Gate National Recreation Area property. The trail continues climbing ever so slightly, snaking through the valley and across several beautiful meadows. One mile from the state park boundary you will encounter a wooden gate that may be open or closed. There are piles of wood, some abandonded cars, etc. From here on is private property and there is no trespassing. Please respect the privacy of the owner. Turn back and coast virtually all the way to the intersection with the Riding and Hiking Trail. Here you have a choice. Either retrace your route completely back to Sir Francis Drake and the park headquarters or bear left on the Riding and Hiking Trail 1.4 miles to the Madrone Group Camp and then out onto Sir Francis Drake and the park headquarters.

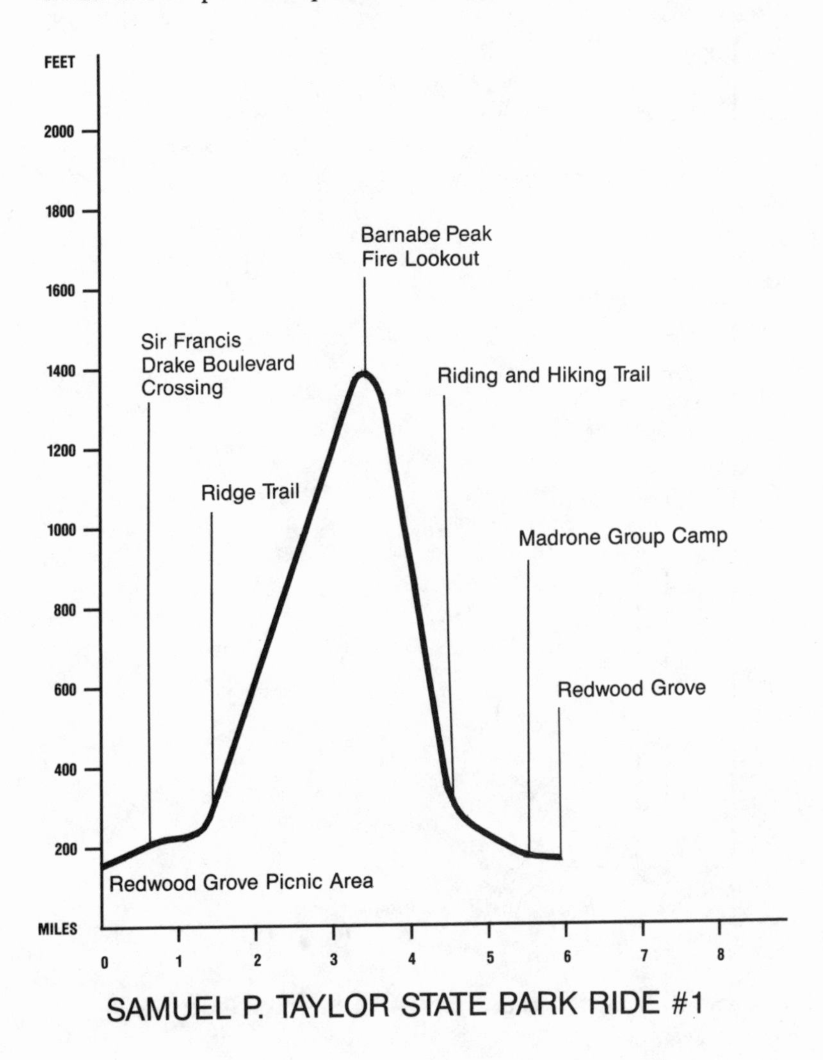

SAMUEL P. TAYLOR STATE PARK RIDE #1

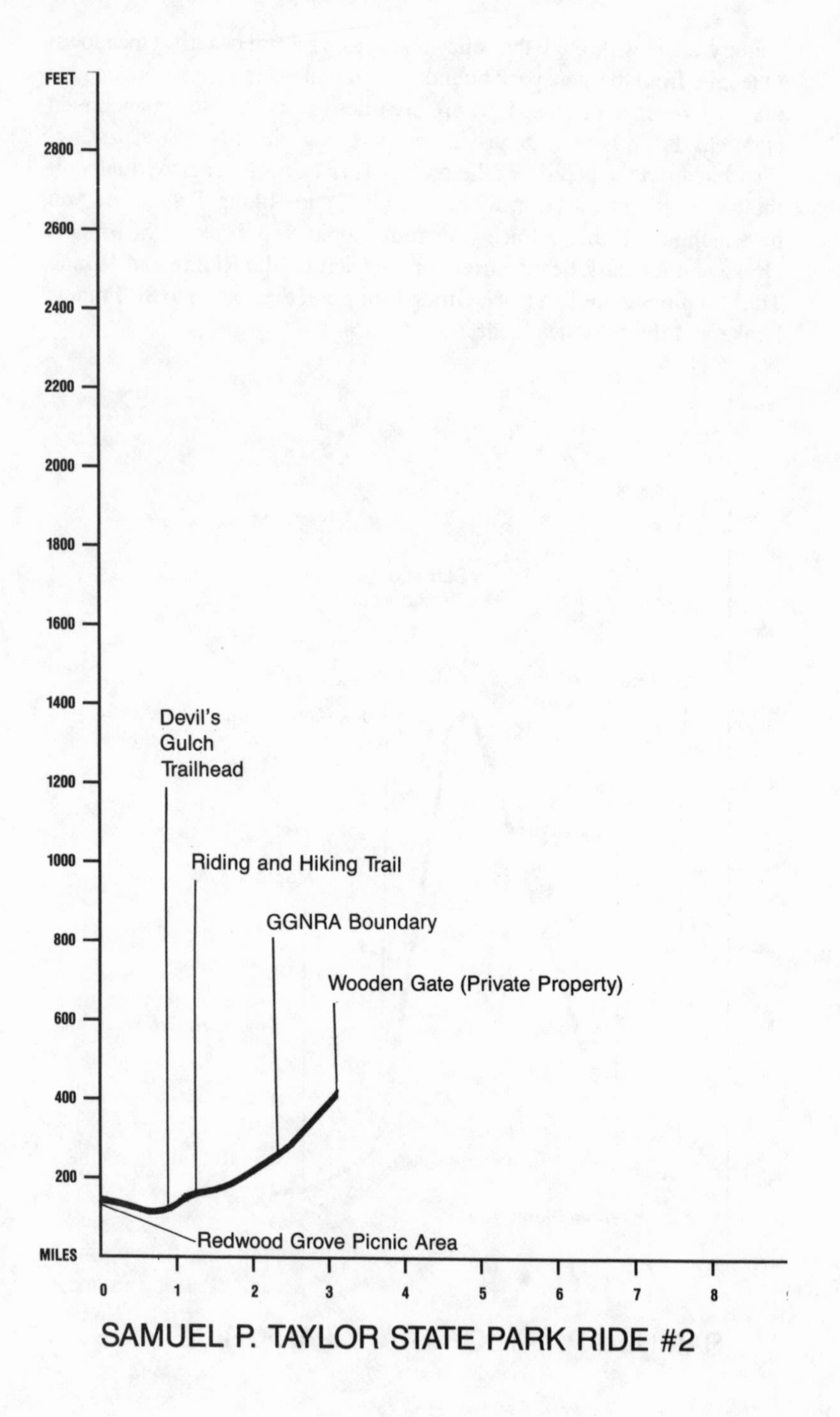

SAMUEL P. TAYLOR STATE PARK RIDE #2

Chapter Five
POINT REYES

Ride #1
TRAILHEAD: *Bear Valley and Rift Zone Trail*
TOPO: *Inverness and Double Point*
OVERALL DIFFICULTY: *Easy*
TECHNICAL DIFFICULTY: *Easy*
DISTANCE: *Approximately 6.2 miles*

Ride #2
TRAILHEAD: *Five Brooks*
TOPO: *Inverness, Double Point, Bolinas, San Geronimo*
OVERALL DIFFICULTY: *Strenuous*
TECHNICAL DIFFICULTY: *Moderately Difficult*
DISTANCE: *Approximately 19 miles*

Highlights

Point Reyes National Seashore is an area that abounds with unique geological and natural phenomena. The area rides precariously on the eastern edge of the Pacific plate, which accounts for the fact that the rocks in Point Reyes match those of the Tehachapi Mountains 310 miles to the south. A ''belt'' of topographic changes and distinct features follow the San Andreas Fault, which runs up the Olema Valley, near park headquarters. In the great earthquake of 1906, the peninsula, hinging upon the Olema Valley, was moved forcefully 20 feet northwestward.

In the spring, mild weather and carpets of wild flowers grace the folded landscape. There are miles of beaches and Douglas fir and Bishop pine forests that stretch to the ocean. Quite often deer are seen browsing among sea lions basking in the sun. During the winter months it is possible to view migratory gray whale just offshore; often the beaches and bays are filled with seals and a wide variety of shore birds. Take your binoculars and enjoy.

There is quite a varied history to be found in this land as well. First inhabited by the Coast Miwok Indians, the area was hunted and harvested peacefully. During the summer of 1579 Sir Francis Drake, an English adventurer, landed here and claimed this land for England and Queen Elizabeth. The English never came back to defend their claim, instead leaving it for the Spaniards to colonize in 1769; during this period, the Miwok Indians had all but been removed from their native land to labor in Spanish missions, and Point Reyes was inhabited by the Miwoks no longer. Word of the the richness of pelts and resources of the area reached many distant nations. This wide influence from the outside world upon the settlers of California and Mexico in part led them to revolt against Spain and establish an independent Republic of Mexico in 1821. The United States takeover of California led to a breakup of large land holdings into numerous cattle ranches. Beef and dairy cattle have wandered Point Reyes ever since. Congress passed legislation protecting Point Reyes as a National Seashore on September 13, 1962.

Within the boundaries there is no car camping. However there are four hike-in campgrounds that are available without charge at Bear Valley Visitor Center.

Getting There

Take the Francis Drake exit off 101 just south of the intersection of Interstate 580 and Highway 101 and north of the Golden Gate Bridge. Travel east on Francis Drake, passing through the towns of Kentfield and Fairfax, past Samuel P. Taylor State Park (a great place to base camp if you are staying overnight; another great camping area is to the east of Pt. Reyes), to Olema and the intersection with Highway 1. Turn right on Highway 1 and bear left almost immediately on Bear Valley Road. There is a mountain bike rental shop on the corner here called Trail Head Rentals. Its number is 415-663-1958. Once on Bear Valley Road travel about .5 mile to the park headquarter's entrance and a left turn. Park in the clearly marked visitor parking near the headquarters.

Ride #1

This ride begins to the south or far end of the parking area at the trailhead for the Rift Zone Trail and the Bear Valley Trail. The Rift Zone branches off to the left and is illegal for mountain bikes. An easy .2-mile pedal will take you to the intersection with the Sky Trail, also illegal for mountain bikes, branching off to the right. Numerous hikers and other bikers will

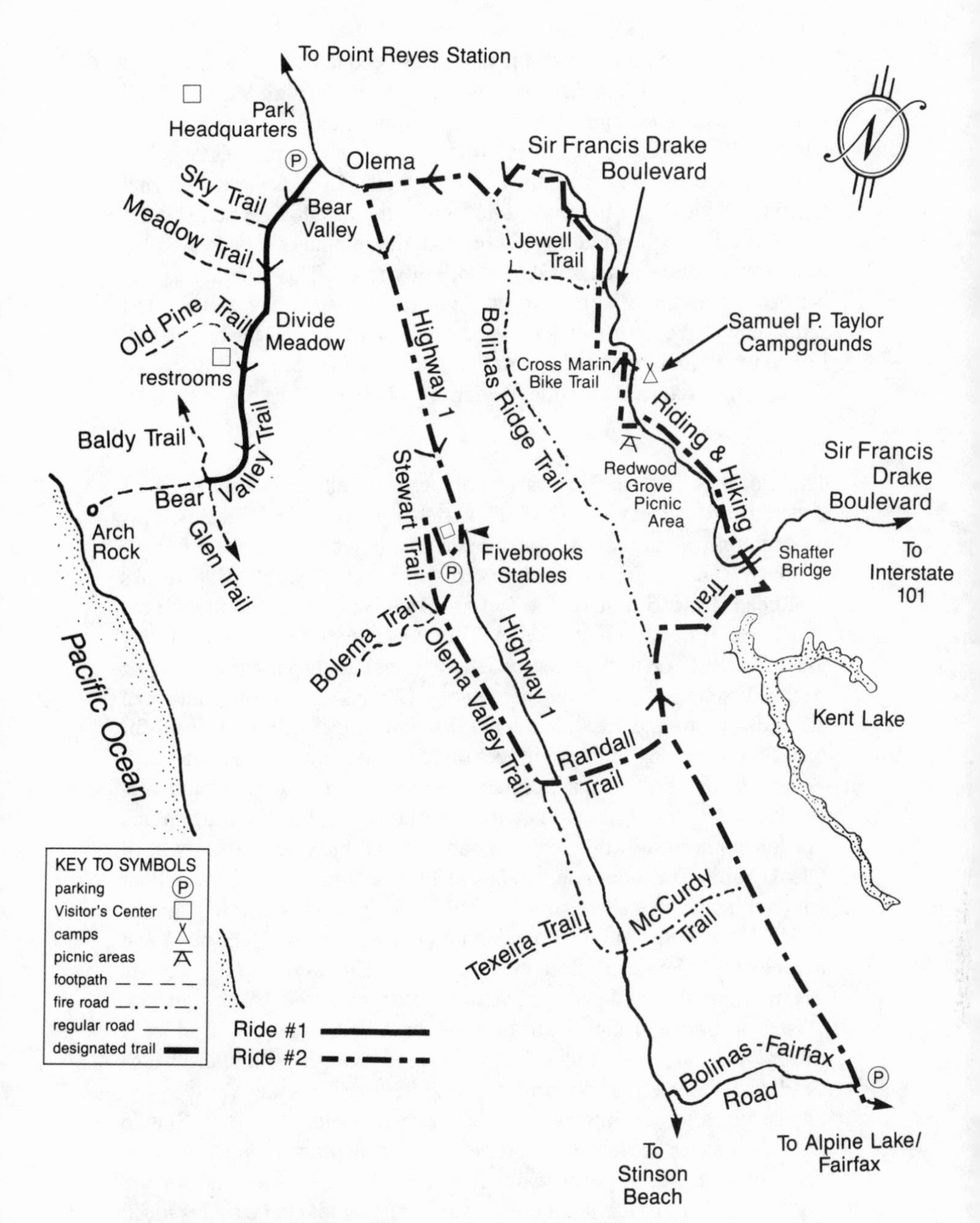

POINT REYES RIDES #1 & #2

be encountered on this beautiful ride; please pedal slowly and always in control. Continue straight .6 mile past the intersection with Meadow Trail branching right and begin a gentle uphill climb .8 mile to Divide Meadow, Old Pine Trail to the right, and restrooms. Spend a few minutes here taking in the scenery and, perhaps if you are lucky like we were, enjoying a generous view of a bobcat gliding across the meadow. When you are ready, head straight and downhill through dense pines and a cool valley to the intersection of Bear, Glen, and Baldy trails. This is as far as you can ride; note the bike rack to the right for cyclists' convenience. The remaining trail crosses wilderness preserve and is illegal for bicycles. It is well worth locking your bike for the brief jaunt down to Arch Rock and the beach. To return back to the parking area, head back the way you came.

Ride #2

This ride may be started in a variety of locations: either Samuel P. Taylor State Park, Point Reyes Park Headquarters, or Fivebrooks Stables. This description will start at the parking area for Fivebrooks Stables just off Highway 1, beginning at the large dirt parking area and the Fivebrooks Trailhead. Ride .3 mile on the Stewart Trail to the intersection with the Rift Zone Trail and Olema Valley Trail. Bear left on the Olema Valley Trail. You will pass through several intersections closely packed and leading back to Fivebrooks Stable, but continue on Olema Valley. Grunt and groan 1.2 miles up to and past the intersection with Bolema Trail (illegal for bicycles) branching to the right; continue to the left on the Olema Trail. From here the trail rolls and descends predominantly on sandy and silty single track to the intersection with Randall Trail 1.3 miles away. Watch out for gopher holes that suddenly appear and bury your front wheel! Olema Valley Trail continues straight to Texeira Trail 2.3 miles away. Bear left, continuing on the Olema Valley Trail, and descend .4 mile to Highway 1. The start of Randall Trail begins immediately across Highway 1 and ascends for 1.7 miles to Bolinas Ridge Trail. The climb is terraced and steady; downshift and pace your climb and try practicing your mantras.

Once at Bolinas Ridge Trail, proceed through the gate and head left 1 mile to the intersection with Shafter Bridge Trail. The Shafter Bridge Trailhead is somewhat concealed and to the right, so stay alert; it will appear just after leaving the cover of trees and a short downhill. Should you encounter a cattle gate you have gone too far; turn around and look carefully for the trail now on your left. Shafter Bridge is a wild and whooping downhill rush 1.9 miles away. Stay in control; though the trail is mostly hard-pack, there are some loose spots that could make things a little more exciting than planned. At the bottom of the descent, a trail branches off to the right and toward the dam. Head straight, toward Shafter Bridge

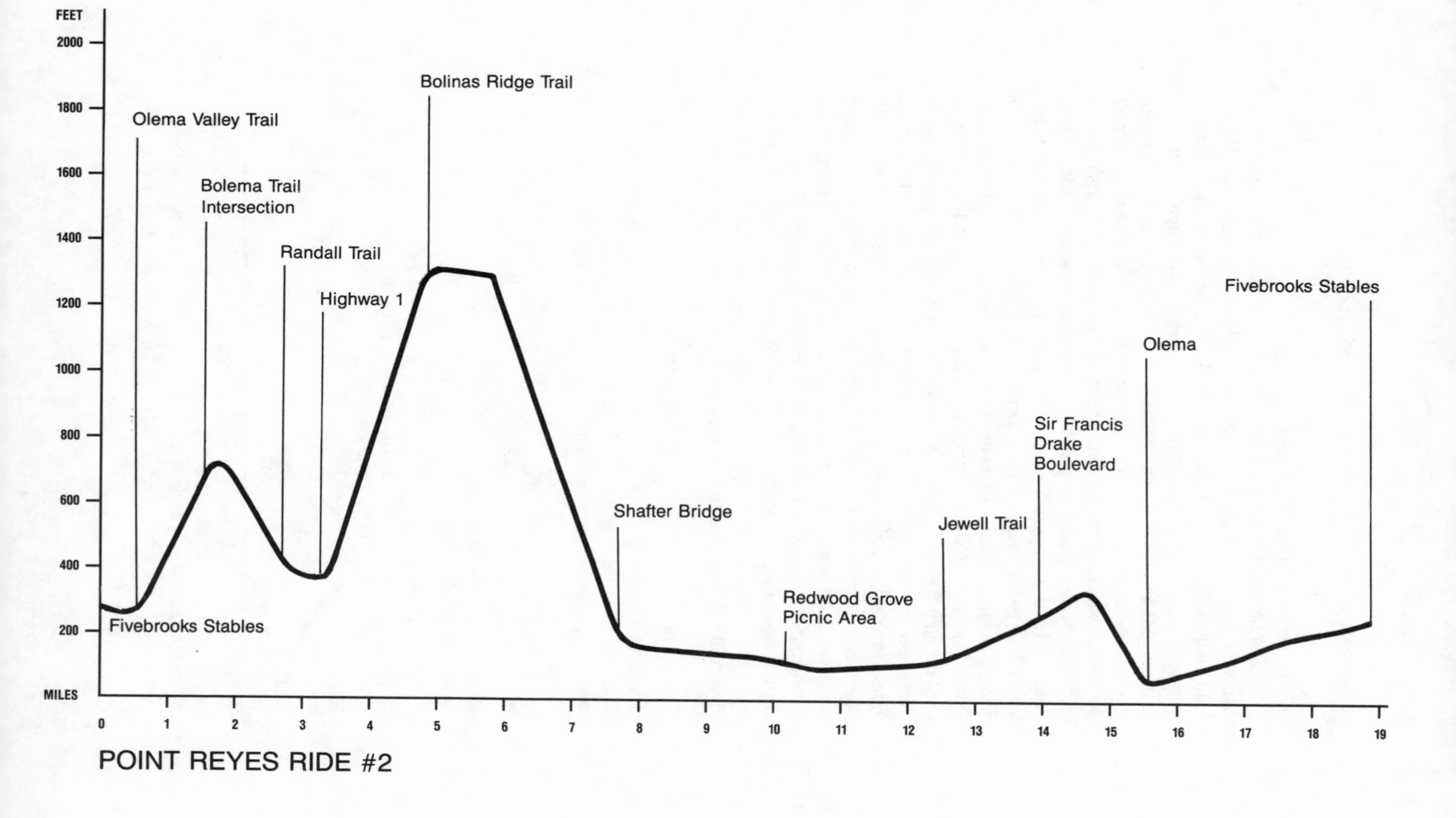

POINT REYES RIDE #2

and Sir Francis Drake Boulevard.

Once at Shafter Bridge you have two options. We recommend picking your way on an unmarked trail under the bridge to the Riding and Hiking Trail on the other side of Papermill Creek. Bear left on the trail and ride 1.9 miles to the Irvine Picnic Area and a pedestrian bridge crossing Sir Francis Drake Boulevard. The route under Shafter Bridge may get your feet wet and is somewhat tricky; however, it avoids Sir Francis Drake Boulevard, which can be quite busy with cars and RVs. If you wish to avoid carrying your bike and crossing the creek, turn left on Sir Francis Drake Boulevard and ride approximately 1.9 miles to rejoin the Riding and Hiking Trail at Irvine Picnic Area and cross over the road on the pedestrian bridge. Pedal .5 mile to the Redwood Grove Picnic Area and Samuel P. Taylor State Park. Continue straight, past the campgrounds on a service road through the state park. The service road becomes a paved bicycle trail which you will follow past the intersection with Jewell Trail at 2.2 miles. Proceed straight on the paved bicycle trail to Sir Francis Drake Boulevard 1.5 miles away and a left turn. The remaining 5.1-mile portion of this ride is on public highway — remember to use extreme caution. Pedal up and out of the canyon 1.8 miles on Sir Francis Drake Boulevard to the town of Olema and the intersection with Highway 1. At Olema turn left and ride a rolling 3.3 miles on Highway 1 to the gravel turnoff for Fivebrooks Stables and the parking area.

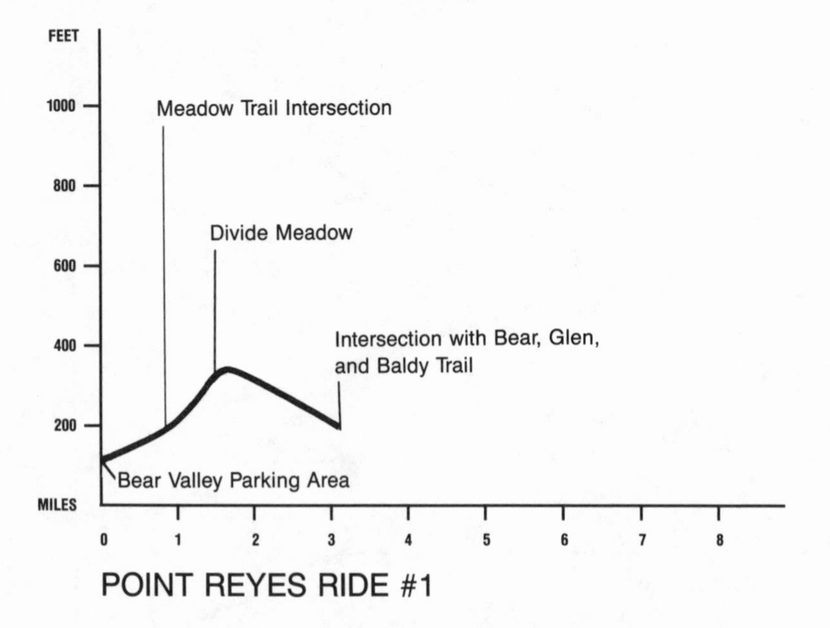

POINT REYES RIDE #1

Chapter Six

ANNADEL STATE PARK

Ride #1
TRAILHEAD: *North Burma Trail, Channel Drive*
TOPO: *Santa Rosa*
OVERALL DIFFICULTY: *Moderate*
TECHNICAL DIFFICULTY: *Moderate/Difficult*
DISTANCE: *8.6 miles*

Ride #2
TRAILHEAD: *Schultz Trail, Schultz Road*
TOPO: *Kenwood*
OVERALL DIFFICULTY: *Moderate*
TECHNICAL DIFFICULTY: *Moderate*
DISTANCE: *7.2 miles*

Ride #3
TRAILHEAD: *Schultz Trail, Schultz Road*
TOPO: *Kenwood and Santa Rosa*
OVERALL DIFFICULTY: *Moderate/Strenuous*
TECHNICAL DIFFICULTY: *Moderate*
DISTANCE: *13.5 miles*

Highlights

Nestled in Sonoma County, Annadel State Park's 5,000 acres of rolling, rocky terrain offer the visitor a stunning collage of intermittent streams, verdant meadows, and quiet woodlands.

The area was first frequented by the Southern Pomo and the Southern

Wappo Indian tribes. Though no permanent villages were established, the rocky hills were important to the Indians as a source of obsidian, which they fashioned into scrapers, knives, arrowheads, and spear points. After 1770, the Spanish introduced farming and cattle ranching, which began replacing the Indian influence of hunting and gathering in the area. In 1837, Annadel became part of a 19,000-acre Mexican land grant. Beginning in the 1880s, as San Francisco and other west coast cities were being built, sheep and cattle grazing in the vicinity was replaced by the demand for cobblestone material. A plentiful resource at Annadel, cobblestone quarrying became a major income source for several families. The granddaughter of one of the families even had the area named after her, "Annie's Dell," which later became the inspiration for the name of the park, Annadel.

When the demand for cobblestone faded in the 1920s the land reverted back to agricultural use. Periodically, perlite, a derivative of obsidian used as insulation, was mined. The area was purchased and designated a state park in 1971.

You will experience a wide range of environmental conditions within the park's boundaries—Douglas fir, chaparral, oaks, redwoods, and open meadows. This diversity affords the visitor a unique opportunity to view a tremendous variety of birds and other wildlife. The best months to view wildflowers are April and May, although many plants bloom beginning in January and continue until September.

Getting There

Located near the city of Santa Rosa just east of Interstate 101. From San Francisco take 101 north to Highway 12 exit. Follow Highway 12 through Santa Rosa to Los Alamos Road. Turn right on Los Alamos to Channel Drive. Head left on Channel Drive to the park headquarters and a small parking area on the right. From the East Bay you will follow Interstate 80 to Highway 29 toward Napa. Just after the junction of Highway 221 and 29 bear right on Highway 12/121. Remain on Highway 12 through Sonoma and Kenwood. Shortly after passing through Kenwood you will turn left on Los Alamos Road and then left on Channel Drive.

Ride #1

Beginning at the small parking area by the park headquarters, bear right on Channel Drive, pedal .3 mile, and turn right on North Burma Trail. The trail climbs quickly through a boulder-strewn path; it may be necessary to dismount and walk your bike over some large rocks. After 1.5 miles of this technical challenge and uphill effort is the intersection with Live Oak Trail. Bear right on Live Oak and ride .4 mile across open and level

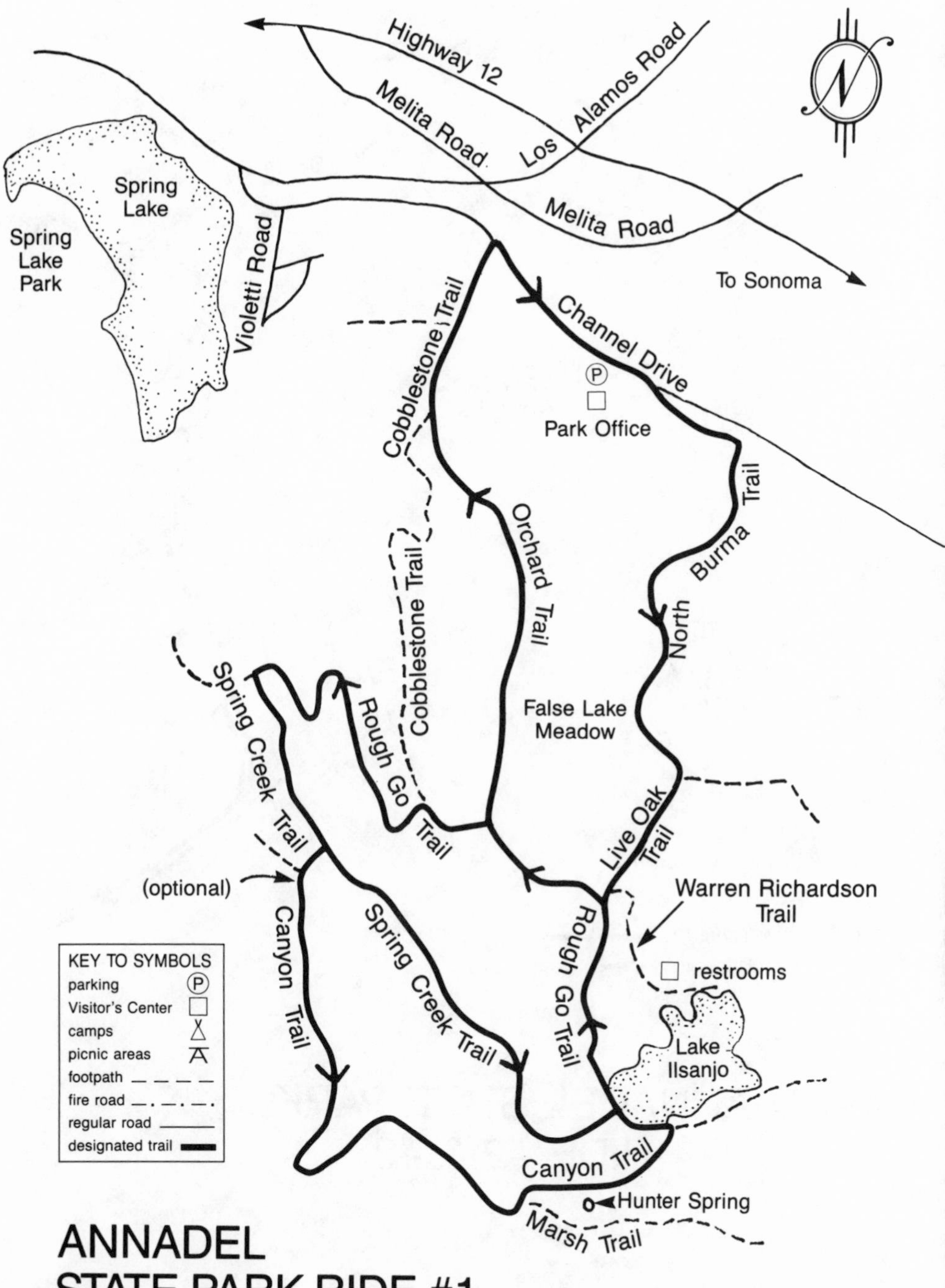

ANNADEL STATE PARK RIDE #1

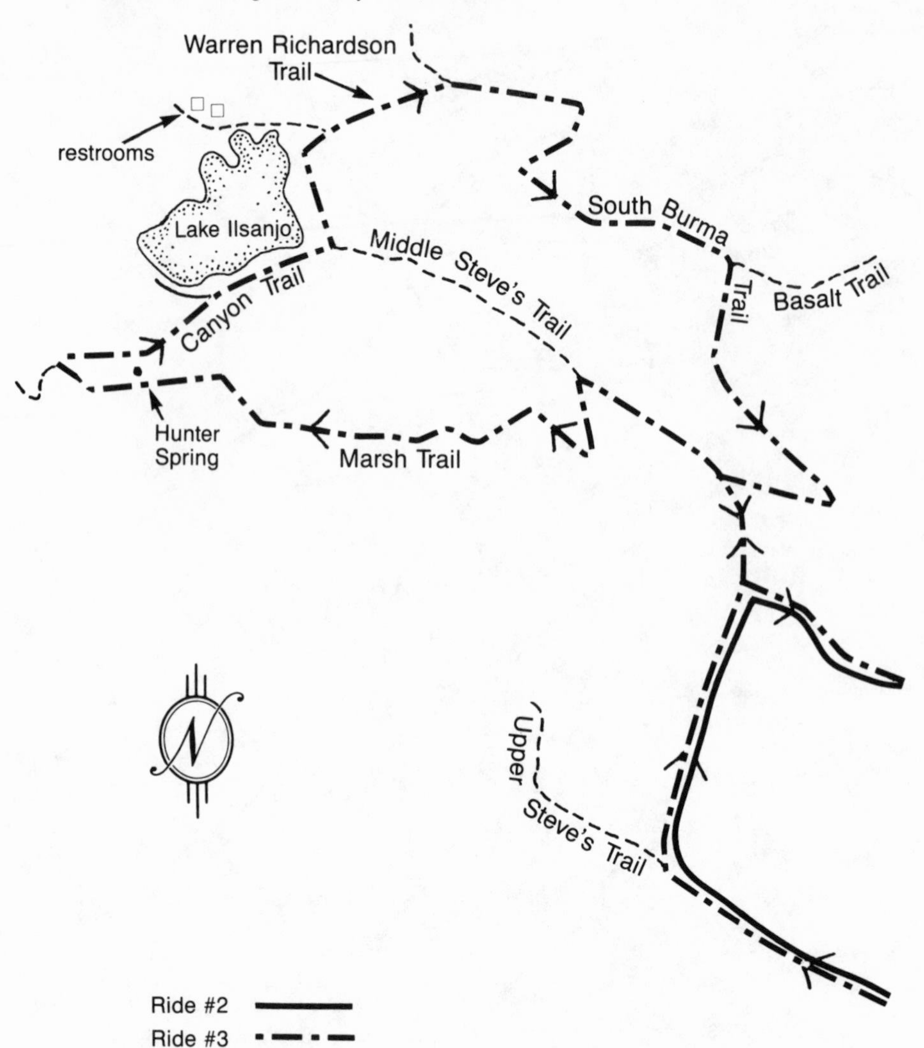

ANNADEL STATE PARK
RIDE #2 & #3

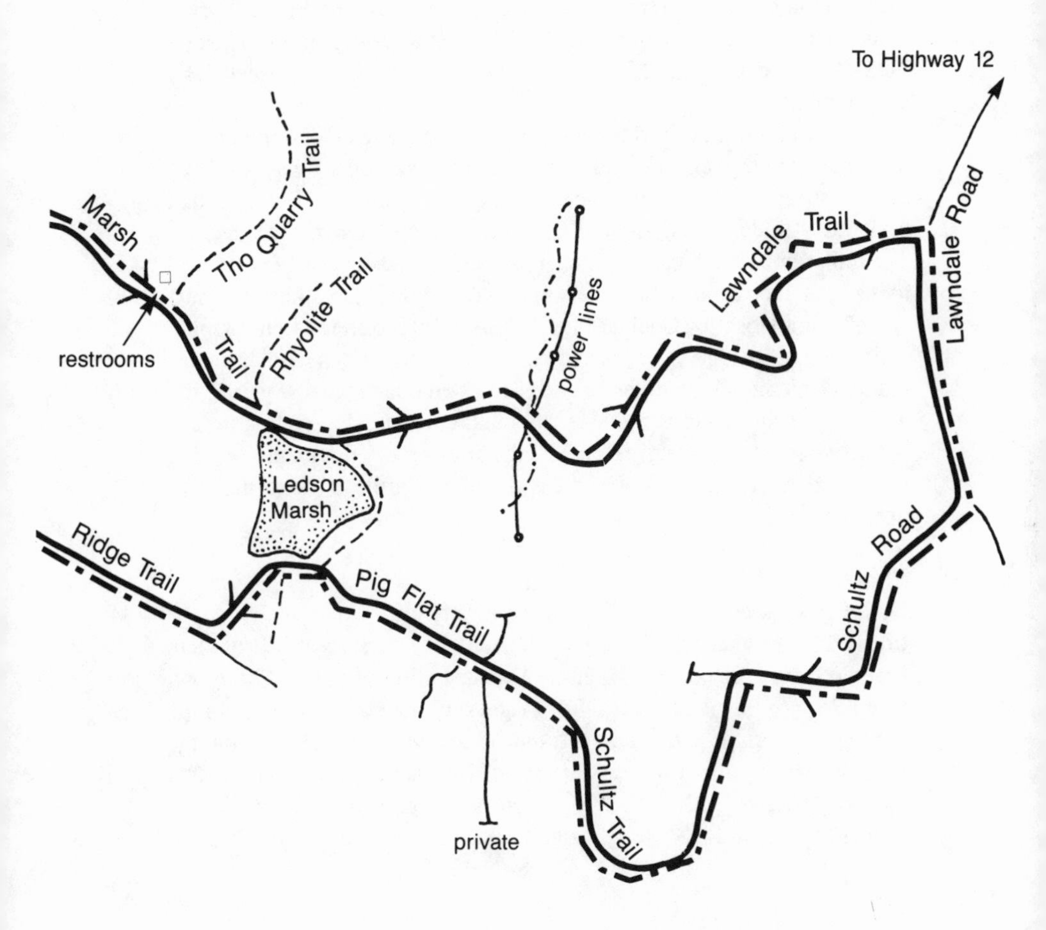
KEY TO SYMBOLS
parking
Visitor's Center
camps
picnic areas
footpath
fire road
regular road
designated trail
To Highway 12
Marsh Trail
Tho Quarry Trail
Rhyolite Trail
restrooms
power lines
Lawndale Trail
Lawndale Road
Ledson Marsh
Ridge Trail
Pig Flat Trail
Schultz Road
Schultz Trail
private

meadow to the intersection with Rough Go Trail and Warren Richardson Trail. Turn right on Rough Go and begin to gain firsthand knowledge of why this trail was named "Rough Go." The next 1.5 miles may turn your knuckles white, jar your kidneys, and stretch your level of sanity. Take this very, very rocky descent slowly and look for a path between the rocks. After .3 mile you will pass the intersection with Orchard Trail to the right. Remember this cutoff, as you will later follow it for the return trip to your car. Continue straight on Rough Go, passing Cobblestone after .2 mile, to Spring Creek Trail 1 mile later.

Head left on Spring Creek for .5 mile of level cycling to the intersection with Canyon Trail heading right. Here you have an option. You can continue straight on Spring Creek, climbing gently 1.3 miles to the intersection with Rough Go Trail at the dam and overlooking Lake Ilsanjo. Or bear right on Canyon Trail, climb steadily past the intersection with Marsh Trail and picnic area at 1.6 miles, descend .6 mile, passing Hunter Spring to the intersection with Rough Go Trail. Here you will bear left, skirting Lake Ilsanjo, and pedal .2 mile across the dam to the Spring Creek Trail intersection.

Either way, once at the dam, head straight on Rough Go .5 mile to the intersection with Warren Richardson and Live Oak trails. Rough Go lives up to its name again as you bear left on the .3-mile section you had previously ridden. Bear right at Orchard Trail and across the meadow. The trail climbs and dips, sometimes suddenly (Michael was reintroduced to his bike's top tube during one sudden, root-filled transition), the next 1.1 miles until meeting Cobblestone Trail. At Cobblestone descend .8 mile. (There is one confusing section to beware of. You will encounter an unmarked trail branching to the left and across an open meadow toward the west and Spring Lake Park. Stay right and continue descending toward the housing developments below.) At the housing developments you will rejoin Channel Drive. Bear right and pedal .4 mile back to the park headquarters.

Rides #2 & #3
Getting There

Located near the city of Santa Rosa just east of Interstate 101. From San Francisco take 101 north to Highway 12 exit. Follow Highway 12 through Santa Rosa to Lawndale Road. Turn right on Lawndale and drive to the parking area on the right and the trailhead for Lawndale Trail. From the East Bay you will follow Interstate 80 to Highway 29 toward Napa. Just after the Highway 221 and 29 junction bear right on Highway 12/121. Remain on Highway 12 through Sonoma and Kenwood. Shortly after pass-

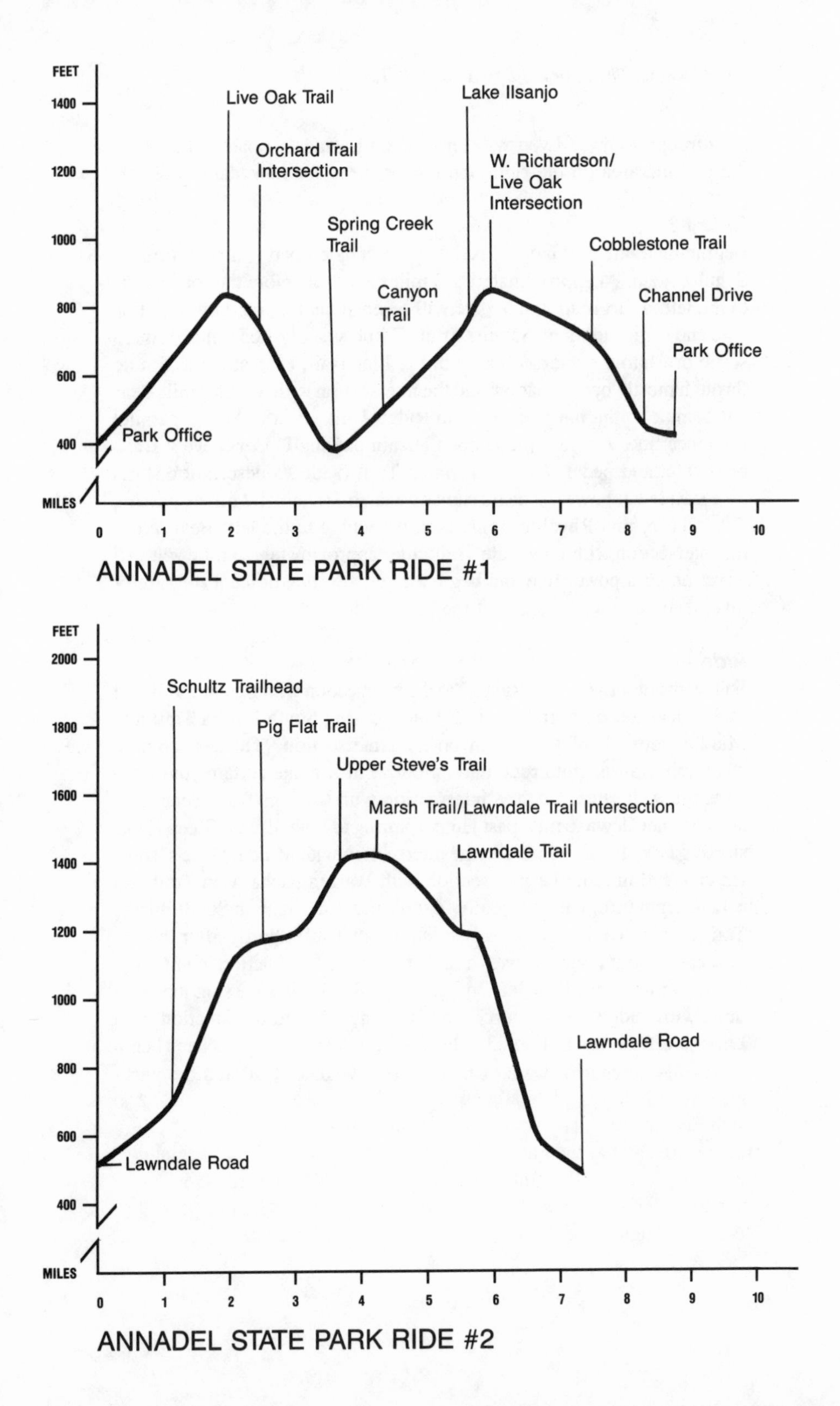
FEET
1400
1200
1000
800
600
400
MILES
0
1
2
3
4
5
6
7
8
9
10
Live Oak Trail
Orchard Trail Intersection
Spring Creek Trail
Canyon Trail
Lake Ilsanjo
W. Richardson/ Live Oak Intersection
Cobblestone Trail
Channel Drive
Park Office
Park Office
ANNADEL STATE PARK RIDE #1
FEET
2000
1800
1600
1400
1200
1000
800
600
400
MILES
0
1
2
3
4
5
6
7
8
9
10
Schultz Trailhead
Pig Flat Trail
Upper Steve's Trail
Marsh Trail/Lawndale Trail Intersection
Lawndale Trail
Lawndale Road
Lawndale Road
ANNADEL STATE PARK RIDE #2

ing through Kenwood you will turn left on Lawndale Road and drive to the parking area on the right and the trailhead for Lawndale Trail.

Ride #2

Beginning at the parking lot, pedal up Lawndale Road to a right turn on Schultz Road. At approximately 1.3 miles and just before the road hooks to the left, a dirt road with a gate will be encountered; pass through this gate and begin riding on Schultz Trail. Climb steadily 1.65 miles through scrub brush to the intersection with Pig Flat Trail; head straight .5 mile through mostly open meadow and the intersection with Marsh Trail. Bear left .4 mile to the intersection with Ridge Trail. Turn right and parallel the fence line .7 mile on flat, open terrain passing Upper Steve's Trail; bear right and pedal .7 mile to Marsh Trail (Ride #3 description starts here). Ride #2, however, bears right on Marsh Trail for 1.2 miles, passing Two Quarry and Rhyolite trails, both branching to the left. Bear left at the intersection with Lawndale Trail; after approximately .3 mile you will travel under a power line and begin a rapid 1.5-mile descent (beware of hikers) to Lawndale Road and the parking lot.

Ride #3

Follow the description for Ride #2 to the intersection with Marsh and Ridge trails. Bear left on Marsh Trail .8 mile, passing South Burma Trail and Middle Steve's Trail, to the Canyon Trail intersection. (The next 1.6 mile of Marsh Trail is quite rough and all downhill; make certain your dentures are well glued.) At the intersection with Canyon Trail, bear right and continue down .6 mile past Hunter Spring to Lake Ilsanjo. Keep right, skirting Lake Ilsanjo .3 mile to the intersection with Middle Steve's Trail. Head left .3 mile to the intersection with Warren Richardson Trail and make a right turn. Climb steadily .4 mile and head right on South Burma Trail; climb steadily 1.1 miles past the Basalt Trail. Shortly after this intersection, South Burma levels and then drops to the junction with Marsh Trail, .9 mile later. Bear left on Marsh Trail 1.5 miles passing intersections with Ridge, Two Quarry, and Rhyolite trails to the junction with Lawndale Trail. Ride a level .3 mile, passing under a power line, and begin a 1.5-mile descent (beware of hikers) to Lawndale Road and the parking lot.

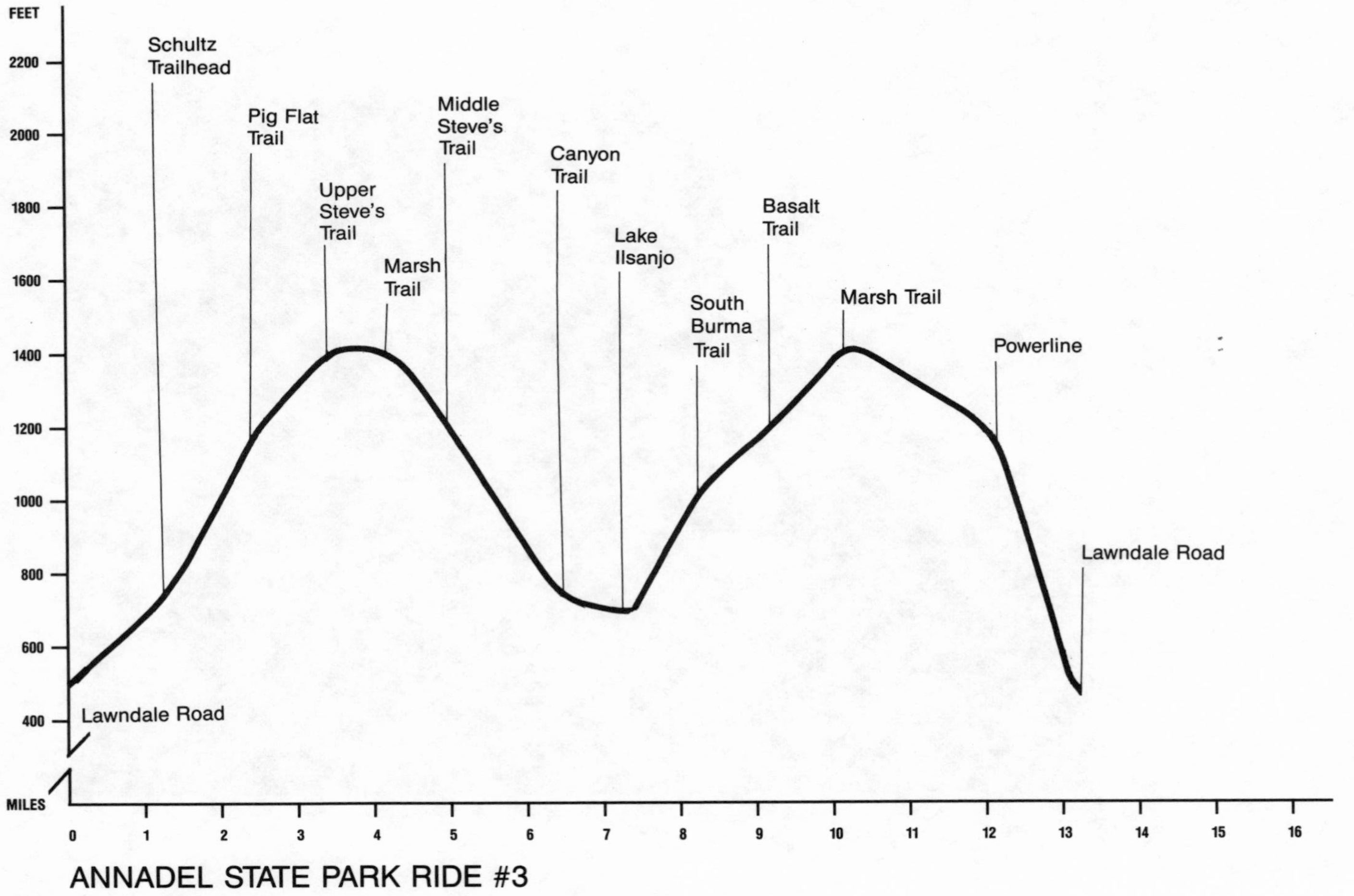

FEET
2200
2000
1800
1600
1400
1200
1000
800
600
400
MILES
0
1
2
3
4
5
6
7
8
9
10
11
12
13
14
15
16
Lawndale Road
Schultz Trailhead
Pig Flat Trail
Upper Steve's Trail
Marsh Trail
Middle Steve's Trail
Canyon Trail
Lake Ilsanjo
South Burma Trail
Basalt Trail
Marsh Trail
Powerline
Lawndale Road
ANNADEL STATE PARK RIDE #3

Chapter Seven

SUGARLOAF STATE PARK

TRAILHEAD: *Ridge View*
TOPO: *Rutherford and Kenwood*
OVERALL DIFFICULTY: *Strenuous*
TECHNICAL DIFFICULTY: *Moderate*
DISTANCE: *6.3 Miles*

Highlights

Sugarloaf State Park extends over 2,500 acres and ranges in elevation from 600 feet at the park entrance to 2,729 feet atop Bald Mountain. Near Annadel State Park and tucked into the wilds of Sonoma County, Sugarloaf is an area widely diverse in plant and wildlife. Whether exploring the high chaparral ridges of Bald Mountain or wandering through the dense groves of trees and sprawling meadows of the Sonoma Creek Drainage, the visitor will find much to enjoy. Some of California's largest bigleaf maple trees can be found here (a good reason to visit in the fall to enjoy the spectacular colors and cooler temperatures) along with madrone, coast redwood, and several varieties of oak. In springtime the area explodes with color from California poppies, cream cups, lupine, penstemon, thistles, buttercups, Indian pinks, brodiaea, and many others. If you travel early, quietly, and with your senses alert, you may have the pleasure of viewing some of the abundant wildlife that this park offers. Blacktail deer, raccoons, bobcats, gray fox, rabbits, squirrels, and weasels all make their home here.

Although the ascent of Bald Mountain is quite strenuous (over 2,100 feet in less than 3 miles), those with the strength and desire will be rewarded with grandeur and a great feeling of accomplishment!

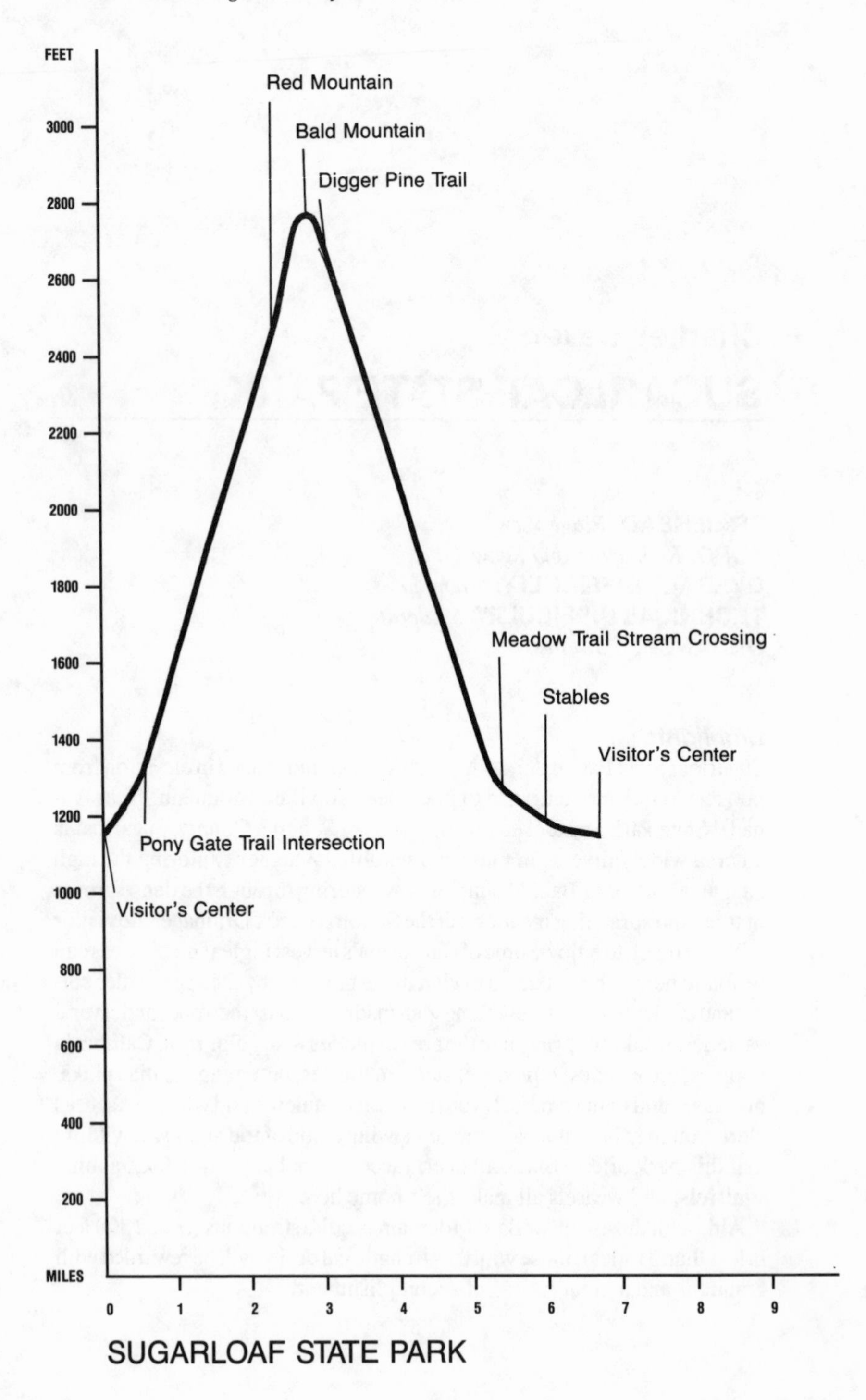

SUGARLOAF STATE PARK

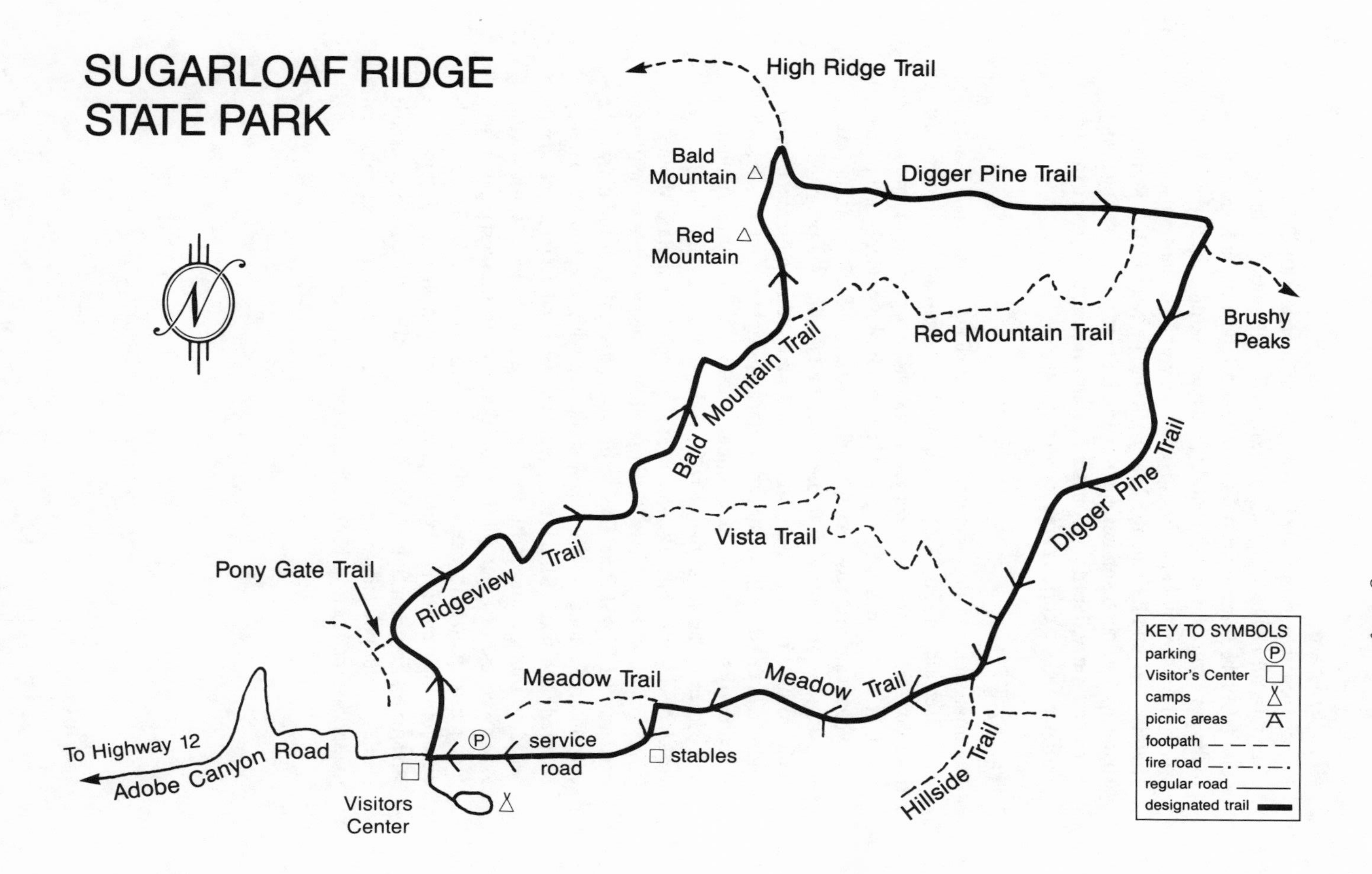
SUGARLOAF RIDGE
STATE PARK
High Ridge Trail
Bald Mountain
Digger Pine Trail
Red Mountain
Red Mountain Trail
Brushy Peaks
Bald Mountain Trail
Digger Pine Trail
Vista Trail
Pony Gate Trail
Ridgeview Trail
Meadow Trail
Meadow Trail
service road
stables
Hillside Trail
To Highway 12
Adobe Canyon Road
Visitors Center
KEY TO SYMBOLS
parking
Visitor's Center
camps
picnic areas
footpath
fire road
regular road
designated trail

Getting There

Located near the city of Santa Rosa just east of Interstate 101. From San Francisco take 101 north to Highway 12 exit. Follow Highway 12 through Santa Rosa to Adobe Canyon Road. Turn left on Adobe Canyon Road and drive to the park entrance and the parking area for all trails. From the East Bay you will follow Interstate 80 to Highway 29 toward Napa. Just after the Highway 221 and 29 junction bear right on Highway 12/121. Remain on Highway 12 through Sonoma and Kenwood. Shortly after passing through Kenwood you will turn right on Adobe Canyon Road and drive to the park entrance and the parking area for all trails.

The Ride

Beginning at the visitor's center, pedal up the Ridge View Trail .5 mile to an intersection with Pony Gate Trail on the left, a dirt road with a no trespassing sign heading straight, and a gate marking the beginning of pavement to the right. Our path is to the right and begins climbing steeply at this point; you will remain on the pavement, rough at times, for 1.8 miles, passing several intersections branching off to the right. At 1.8 miles the pavement continues to the left and a cluster of microwave towers. Although temptation will pull you in this direction, our path will lead us right and up the somewhat ridiculously steep-looking rocky-climb-from-hell. Although the summit has no redeeming features, the view from the top makes the .4-mile ride/walk/crawl worthwhile! We recommend a lunch stop on Bald Mountain's 2,729-foot peak. High Ridge Trail branches to the left while you will descend via the Digger Pine Trail to the right; several brief uphills will be encountered, though they are easy compared with what you have already endured. The next 2.5 miles to a stream crossing and the intersection with Meadow Trail are quite loose, rocky, and rutted with several washouts due to heavy equestrian usage. NOTE: Sugarloaf is one of the most popular areas for equestrians to train for endurance events. Mountain bikers are reminded to remain in control and yield the right-of-way at all times. Just past the stream crossing, bear right on Meadow Trail .8 mile to the Group Camp and stables. At this point leave the trail and bear left heading past the stables on the service road .3 mile back to the parking lot.

Chapter Eight

BRIONES REGIONAL PARK

TRAILHEAD: *Old Briones Road/Bear Creek*
TOPO: *Briones Valley, Walnut Creek*
OVERALL DIFFICULTY: *Moderate/Strenuous*
TECHNICAL DIFFICULTY: *Moderate*
DISTANCE: *Approximately 8.7 miles*

Highlights

Briones Regional Park is a delightfully undeveloped 5,303 acres of rolling grassland, oak woodland, verdant canyons, and hidden meadows. Since the early 1800s much of Briones's history has revolved around cattle ranching. For a short time, during the 1850s and '60s, the Alhambra Valley became an important fruit-growing area with large orchards and vineyards; the gnarled remains of many of these orchards are still evident today. In 1957, Contra Costa County and the East Bay Regional Park District established Briones as a large open space park in the Bear Creek Watershed. With additional annexing of land, the East Bay Regional Park District created a park full of scenic trails perfect for hiking, biking, and equestrian use. This is truly a magical park to explore and enjoy.

Getting There

Located just northwest of Walnut Creek and north of the Caldecott Tunnel on Highway 24. From Highway 24 and the town of Orinda head left on Camino Pablo Road. Drive to Bear Creek Road, where you will turn right, following Bear Creek past Briones Dam to the park entrance.

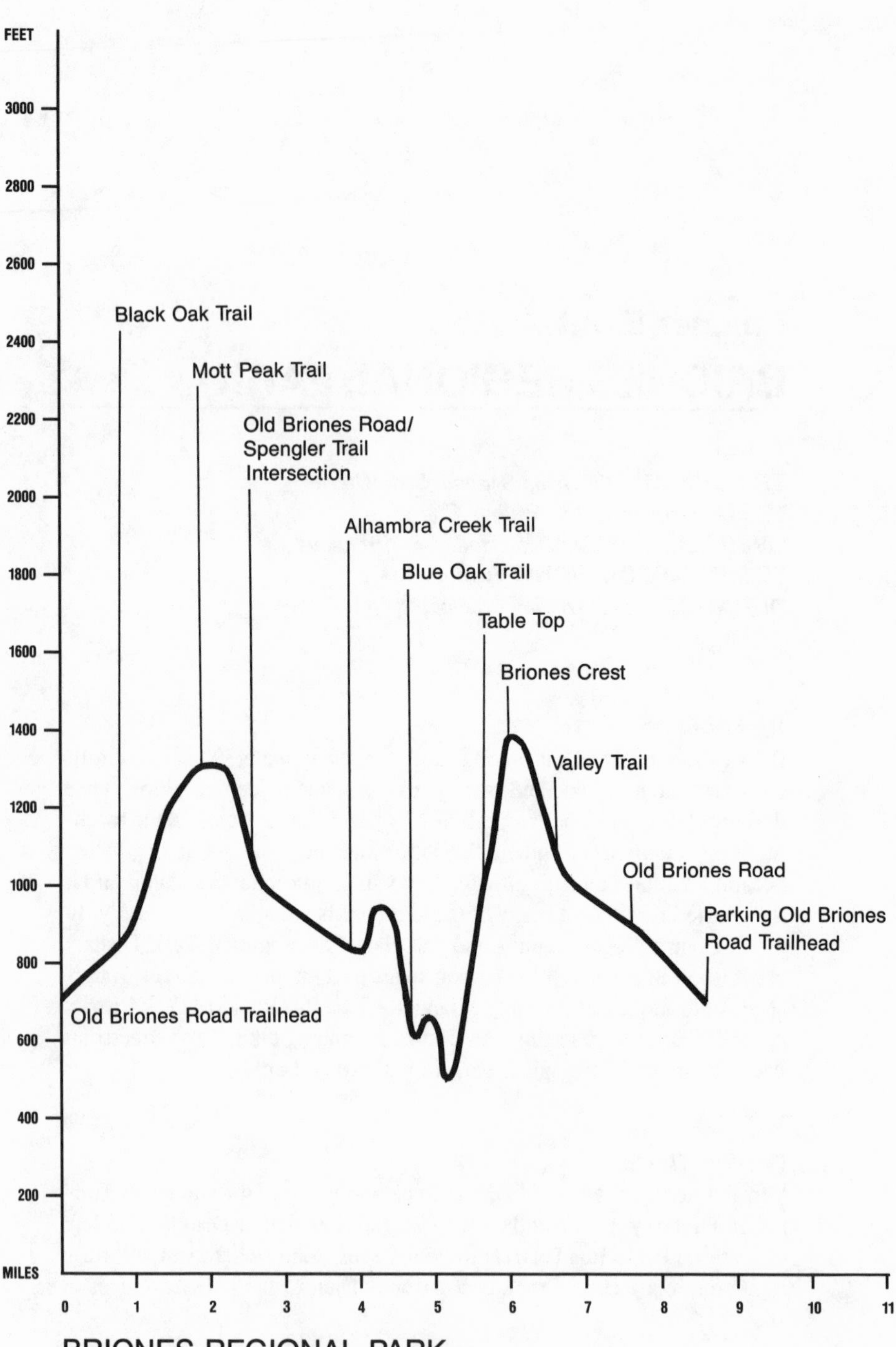

BRIONES REGIONAL PARK

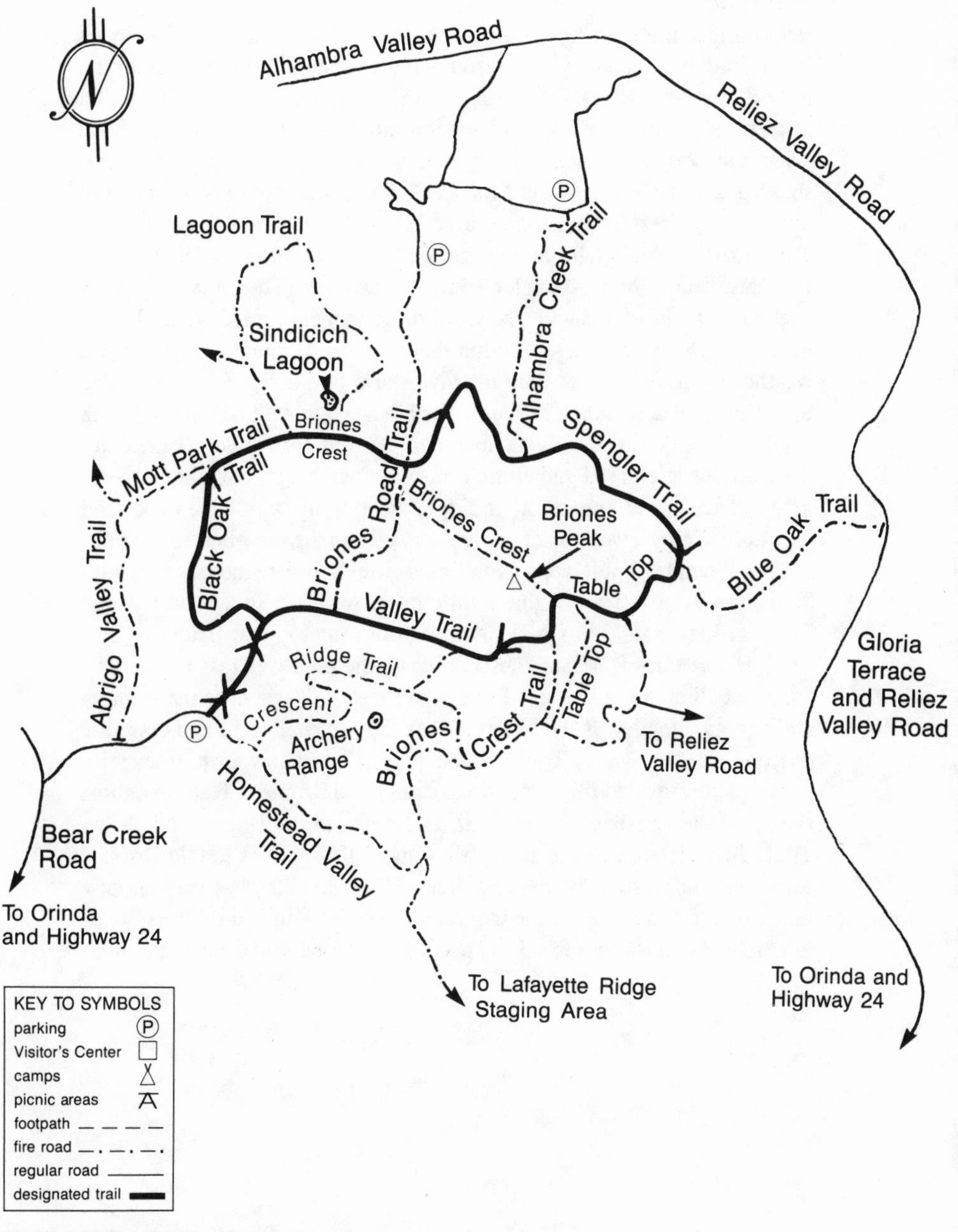

BRIONES REGIONAL PARK

The Ride

Beginning at the Bear Creek entrance and parking area for Old Briones Road Trailhead, pedal .7 mile through a gate and up a slight grade to the intersection with Black Oak Trail. Bear left on the Black Oak Trail and a steep climb—we walked—of several hundred yards to the top of the ridge. The next 1.1 miles are mostly rolling, following the ridge with several sharp ups and downs. At the Mott Peak Trail, turn right and descend to the Briones Crest Trail, .4 mile away. Head right on the Briones Crest Trail, skirting Sindicich Lagoon (more of a cattle wallow) to Old Briones Road and bear right on Spengler Trail, .5 mile away. (The remaining miles back to the parking area will take you through numerous cattle gates. Please be sure to leave them as you found them—closed or open. Also, in wet weather the track can get very muddy—have fun, but use caution.) The Spengler Trail descends 1.2 miles to the intersection with Alhambra Creek Trail. The valley is often very lush and wet but always beautiful. Continue on Spengler Trail and climb over one small ridge, into another very green canyon, and onto another ridge, meeting up with Blue Oak Trail at .7 mile. Enjoy a well-deserved rest and take in the view before continuing on. Spengler Trail drops and climbs quickly before intersecting with Table Top Trail bearing right, 1 mile later. At Table Top, head left and begin a sharp and arduous .5-mile ascent to the top and Briones Crest Trail. Before turning left and descending on the Briones Crest Trail, make the short climb up to Briones Peak (1,483 feet)—if you have the stamina and energy, the view is well worth it. At .5 mile head right and continue descending to the Valley Trail. (If you wish to lengthen your journey with a very picturesque addition, continue straight on Briones Crest, up a short rise, past the Crescent Ridge Trail, and down to the Homestead Valley Trail. Turn right on Homestead Valley and follow it back to Old Briones Road and a left turn to the parking area.) Our path takes us 1 very choppy mile—cattle and horses erode the track when wet—to Old Briones Road. Turn left on Old Briones Road and pedal 1.1 miles back to the parking area.

Chapter Nine
MOUNT DIABLO STATE PARK

RIDE #1
TRAILHEAD: *Wall Point Road, Ranger Station*
TOPO: *Diablo, Las Trampas Ridge, Walnut Creek, Clayton*
OVERALL DIFFICULTY: *Moderate*
TECHNICAL DIFFICULTY: *Moderate*
DISTANCE: *7.3 miles*

RIDE #2
TRAILHEAD: *Wall Point Road, Ranger Station*
TOPO: *Diablo, Las Trampas Ridge, Walnut Creek, Clayton*
OVERALL DIFFICULTY: *Moderately Strenuous*
TECHNICAL DIFFICULTY: *Moderate*
DISTANCE: *13 miles*

RIDE #3
TRAILHEAD: *Deer Flat Road, Juniper Campground*
TOPO: *Clayton*
OVERALL DIFFICULTY: *Strenuous*
TECHNICAL DIFFICULTY: *Moderate*
DISTANCE: *13.3*

Highlights
Standing proudly at the eastern edge of the San Francisco Bay Region, Mount Diablo casts an imposing figure, towering 3,849 feet above the surrounding countryside. No other immediate point in the Central Valley or Coast Range is as high, and the view from on top is nothing short of

spectacular, especially after a winter storm when the air and horizon are clear. With binoculars you can see west to the Golden Gate Bridge and beyond to the Farallon Islands; southeast is 4,213-foot high Mount Hamilton; looking south you can see Loma Prieta peak in the Santa Cruz Mountains; to the north the world opens with views of Mount Saint Helena in the Coast Range; and on a very clear day, to the east is majestic Half Dome in Yosemite National Park.

In 1851, the peak was used by a survey party as a starting point for surveying the surrounding public domain. After erecting a flagpole at the summit, they extended base and meridian lines that we still use today in official land surveys—legal descriptions of real estate throughout much of California and parts of Oregon and Nevada refer to Mount Diablo base and meridian lines. In 1874 toll roads were opened up to the Mount House, a 16-room hotel near the top of the peak. Celebrities from all over the world visited to enjoy sunrise, sunset, and the occasional full moon from the upper slopes of the mountain. In 1891 the summit platform and hotel burned, shortly thereafter leading to the closing of the toll roads; the area then became used mostly for grazing until 1915 when the toll roads were reopened and public access was restored to the peak. In 1921 a small section of mountain was declared a state park and much of the remaining mountain protected as a game refuge. In 1931 the state acquired additional land, and the area was formally dedicated as Mount Diablo State Park.

Getting There

Located just east of Walnut Creek and Interstate 680. From Interstate 680 take Ygnacio Valley Road through the city of Walnut Creek to an intersection with Walnut Avenue. Turn left on Walnut Avenue and drive to the intersection with Oak Grove Road and turn right; proceed several hundred yards and bear left on North Gate Road. Follow North Gate as it winds and climbs into the park and to the headquarters and the intersection with the Summit Road and South Gate Road.

The Ride

Ride #1

Beginning at Wall Point Road trailhead near the ranger station above Rock City, head in a northerly direction (avoid the trail to the right which leads to the summit) toward Dan Cook Canyon Trail, .2 mile away. From the intersection with Dan Cook Trail, head straight, remaining on the Wall Point Road. Descend on a sometimes sandy track 2.5 miles, passing Emmons Canyon Road to the left, and continue .6 mile to the intersection of Pine Canyon Trail and Mount Diablo Trail. Turn right and continue descending toward Pine Creek and a gate crossing at .5 mile. (Ride #2 description begins here and will bear left). Turn right at the gate and begin

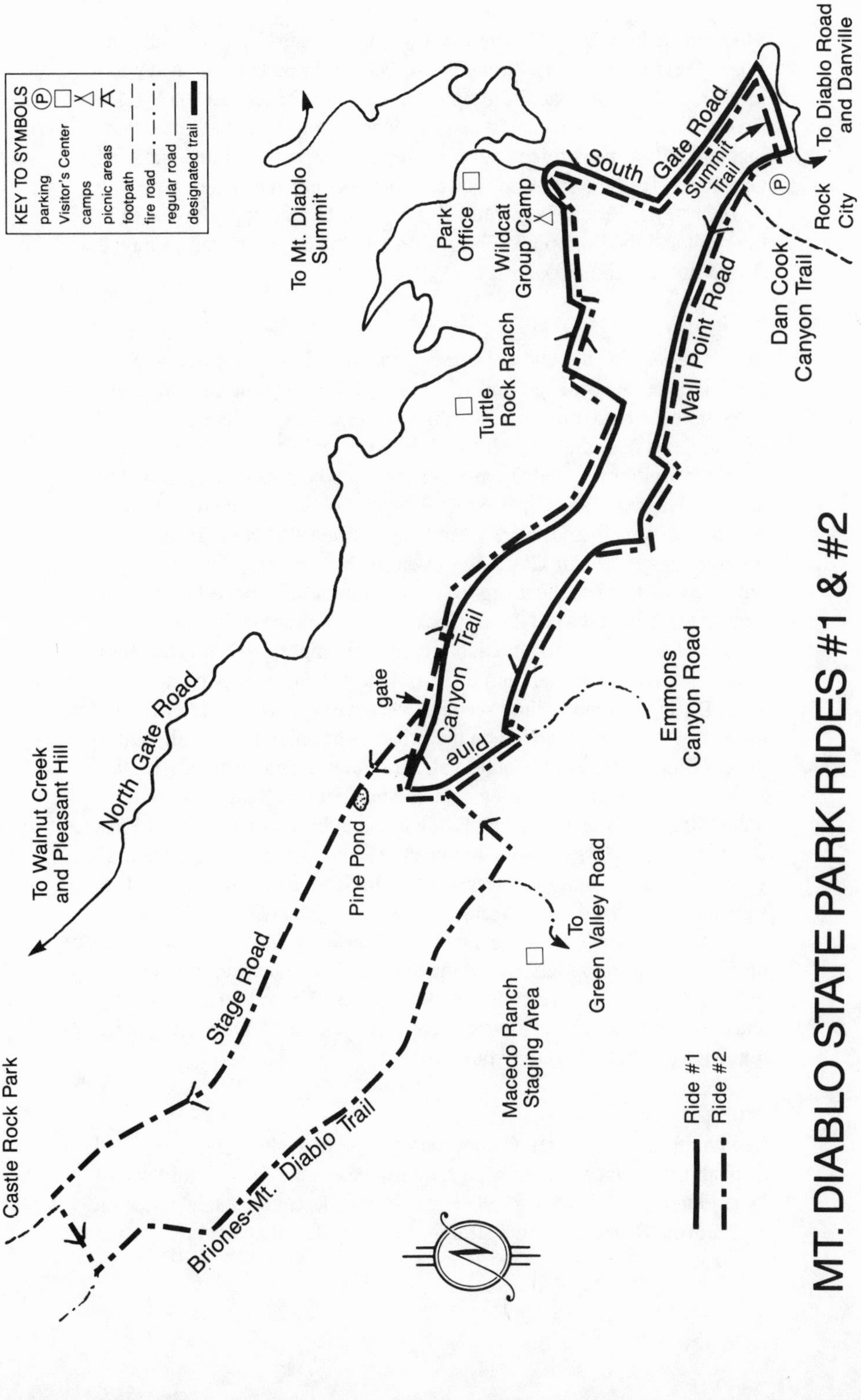

MT. DIABLO STATE PARK RIDES #1 & #2

KEY TO SYMBOLS
parking
Visitor's Center
camps
picnic areas
footpath
fire road
regular road
designated trail

Ride #1
Ride #2

Castle Rock Park
To Walnut Creek and Pleasant Hill
North Gate Road
Stage Road
Briones-Mt. Diablo Trail
Pine Pond
gate
Pine Canyon Trail
Macedo Ranch Staging Area
To Green Valley Road
Emmons Canyon Road
To Mt. Diablo Summit
Turtle Rock Ranch
Park Office
Wildcat Group Camp
Wall Point Road
South Gate Road
Summit Trail
Dan Cook Canyon Trail
Rock City
To Diablo Road and Danville

a long and tedious 2.3-mile climb past Wildcat Group Camp to South Gate Road. This section climbs through some beautiful wooded areas and winds past several private roads leading to Turtle Rock Ranch. At the Wildcat Group Camp Trail intersection, pass through the gate, over the cattle crossing, and follow the service road climbing .2 mile to a right turn on South Gate Road. Traffic on this road can be heavy; beware of vehicles, especially on tight turns. Proceed downhill .9 mile to a large dirt parking area on the right and the Summit Trail. Descend on the Summit Trail .3 mile to Rock City and the parking area.

Ride #2

Beginning at the gate and the intersection with Pine Canyon and Stage Road in Ride #1, bear left and follow the canyon .4 mile to Pine Pond. From here the road turns somewhat messy in spots as it crosses Pine Creek several times. Continue a lush and beautiful .7 mile to the Mount Diablo Park and Diablo Foothills Regional Park boundary, crossing the muddy and challenging Pine Creek several times. At the boundary, the trail becomes dry again and winds .9 mile along the valley and meadows. To the right is spectacular Castle Rock; on the left are rock formations you will encounter before the unsigned intersection near a concrete sluice. To the right takes you toward Castle Rock Park, which at the time of printing is illegal for bikes, although Diablo Park is attempting to acquire access.

Your path takes you left and up .5 mile to the Briones–Mount Diablo Trail. During this short climb keep left when passing through several intersections. At the gate head left on the Briones–Mount Diablo Trail, pedaling a rolling 1.4 miles to another gate; continue .9 mile to an intersection with a road on the right leading out to residential development and Green Valley Road. Head left and up .4 mile to the intersection with Wall Point Road and Pine Canyon Trail. Continue left and down .5 mile on Pine Canyon Trail to a gate and the intersection with Stage Road. At the gate turn right and begin a tedious 2.5-mile climb past Wildcat Group Camp Trail and South Gate Road. Head right on South Gate Road and ride a fast .9-mile descent to a dirt parking area and the Summit Trail connector on the right to Rock City. While on South Gate Road remember to stay alert for RVs and cars barreling around the sharp corners. Descend .3 mile on the Summit Trail to Rock City and your car.

Ride #3

Beginning at the Juniper Campground day-use parking area, proceed through the campground service road loop to a gate for the trailhead of Deer Flat Road. The next .7 mile is a moderate descent to the intersection with Burma Road. Continue straight to Deer Flat; this 1.1-mile section

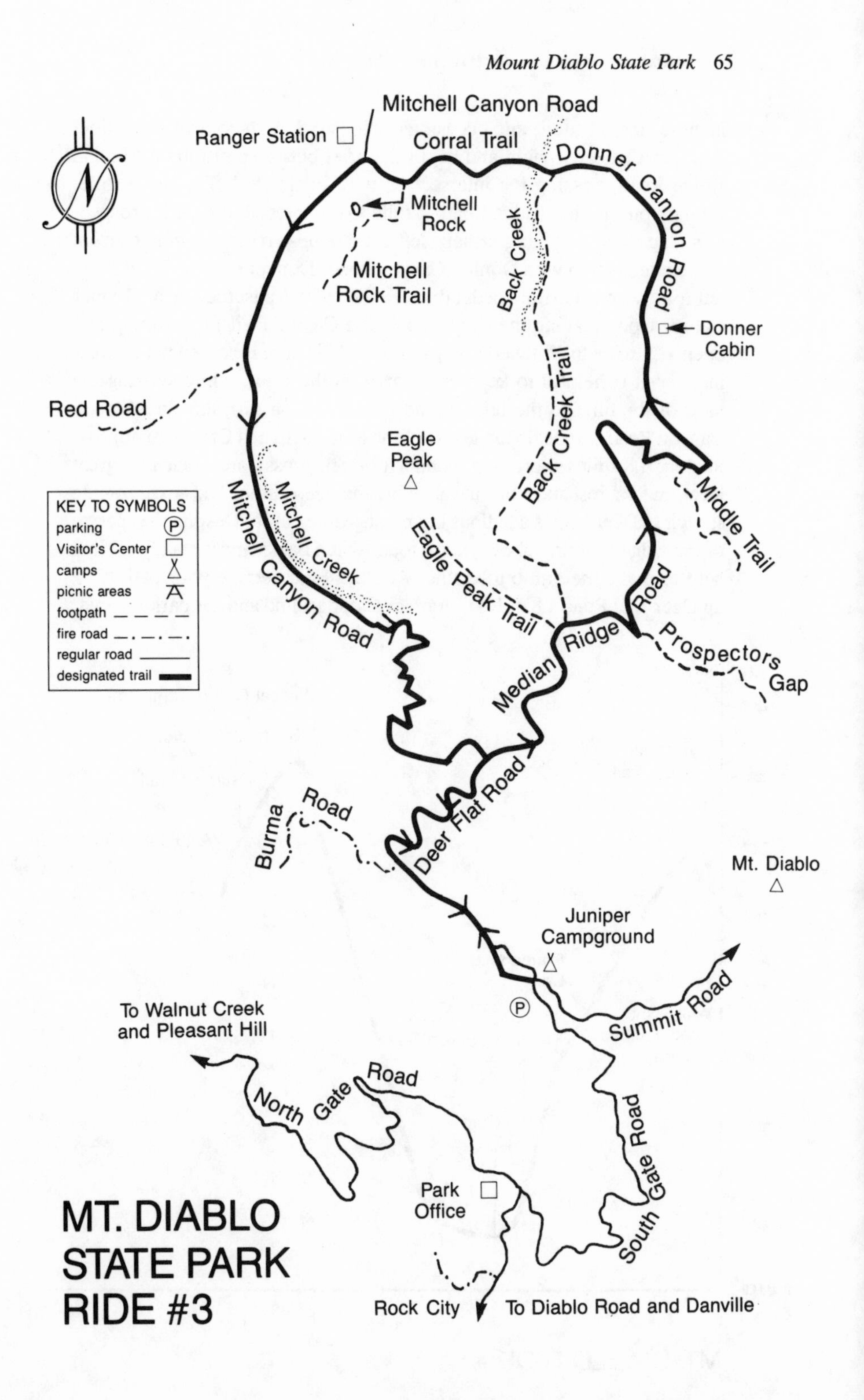
Mitchell Canyon Road
Ranger Station
Corral Trail
Donner Canyon Road
Mitchell Rock
Mitchell Rock Trail
Back Creek
Donner Cabin
Red Road
Eagle Peak
Back Creek Trail
Middle Trail
KEY TO SYMBOLS
parking
Visitor's Center
camps
picnic areas
footpath
fire road
regular road
designated trail
Mitchell Creek
Mitchell Canyon Road
Eagle Peak Trail
Road
Ridge
Prospectors Gap
Median
Deer Flat Road
Burma Road
Mt. Diablo
Juniper Campground
Summit Road
To Walnut Creek and Pleasant Hill
North Gate Road
South Gate Road
Park Office
MT. DIABLO STATE PARK RIDE #3
Rock City
To Diablo Road and Danville

is quite steep, rutted, and occasionally loose. Stay in control and enjoy! At Deer Flat, bear right and begin the brief but steep climb on Median Ridge Road, passing the intersection with Eagle Peak Trail at .8 mile. Remain on Median Ridge Road .4 mile to the intersection with Prospectors Gap Road and hang a sharp left for a bone-jarring 1.5-mile descent to the intersection with Donner Canyon Road. Donner Canyon Road bears left for a scenic 1.8-mile pedal through the canyon past the site of Donner Cabin. Upon leaving the canyon, join the Corral Trail for a rolling and open 1.2 miles to Mitchell Canyon Road. This area is somewhat confusing, but it is helpful to keep the quarry on the right, while skirting the base of the hills to the left. At the ranger station turn left on Mitchell Canyon Road and begin the gentle climb along Mitchell Creek. At approximately 1.8 miles there is a wonderful open grassy area that is a great location for a rest and a bite to eat before the steep climb. The next 2.2-mile stretch to Deer Flat is a tedious but manageable climb. Despite the spectre of the ridge looming above, numerous switch backs and a steady incline help to make the climb tolerable. At Deer Flat, retrace your path back up Deer Flat Road 1.8 miles to Juniper Campground and the parking area.

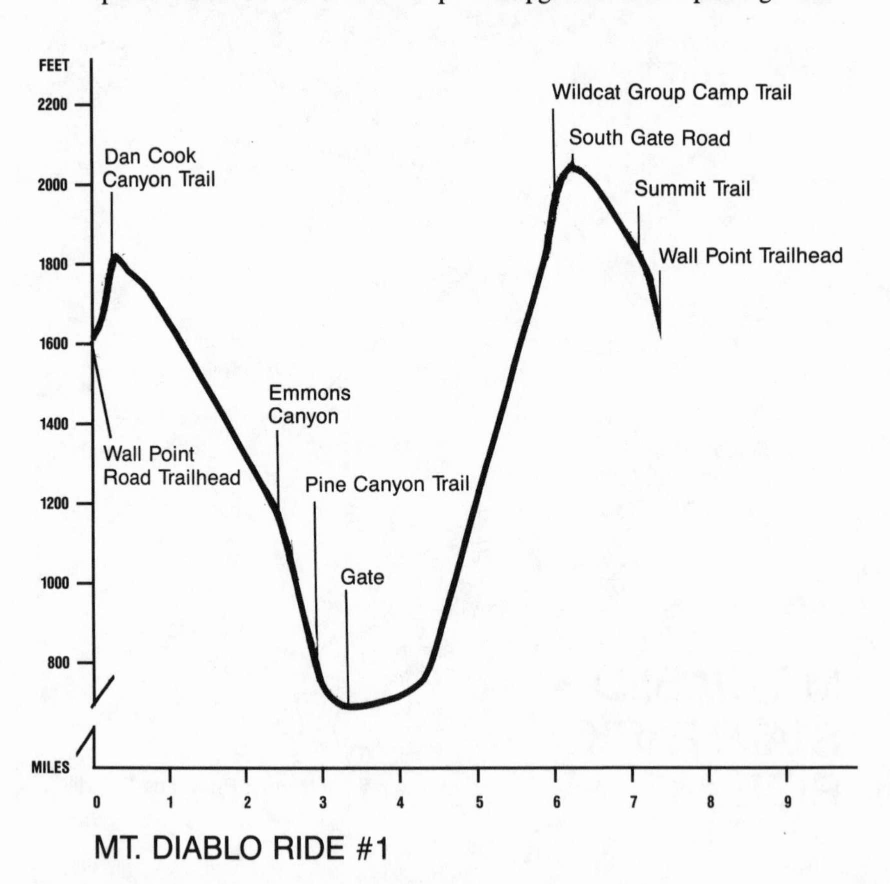

MT. DIABLO RIDE #1

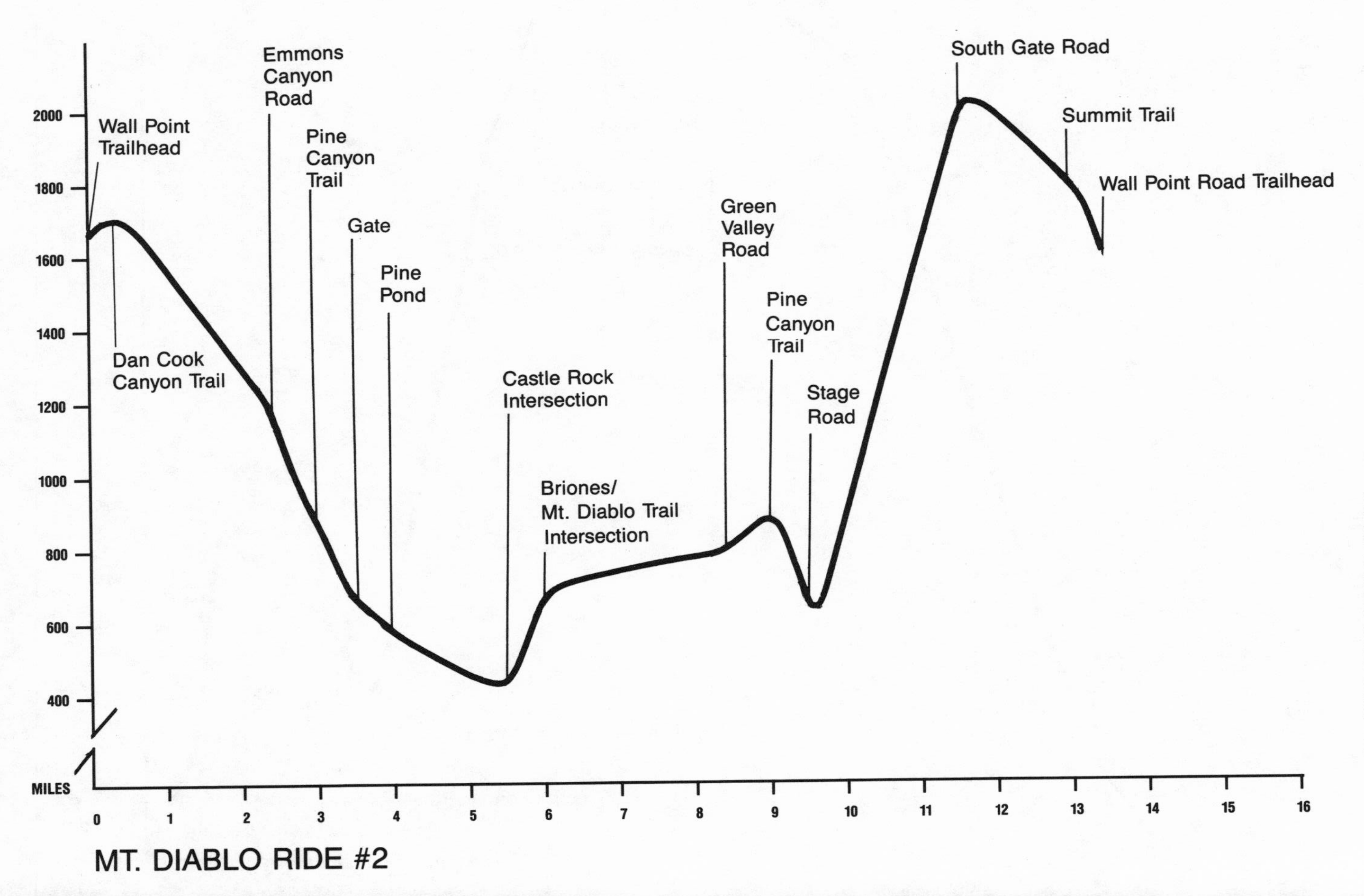

MT. DIABLO RIDE #2

MT. DIABLO RIDE #3

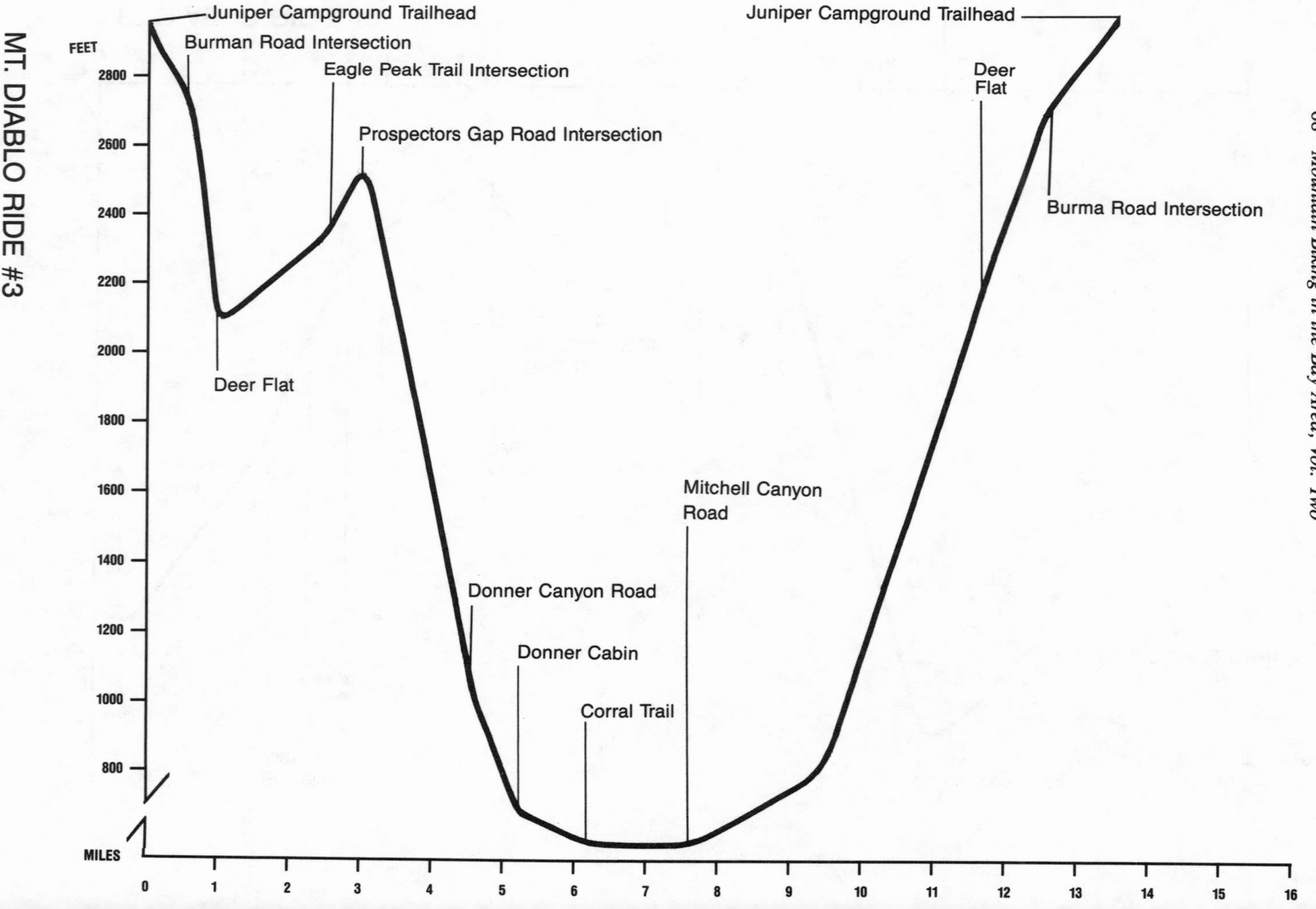

Chapter Ten

WEST TILDEN AND WILDCAT REGIONAL PARK

TRAILHEAD: *Loop Trail, Raccoon Group Camp*
TOPO: *Richmond and Briones Valley*
OVERALL DIFFICULTY: *Moderately strenuous*
TECHNICAL DIFFICULTY: *Moderate*
DISTANCE: *13.3 miles*

Highlights

Called the "crown jewel" of the East Bay Regional Park system, 2,078-acre Tilden Regional Park is indeed a gem. Established in 1936, it is one of the oldest in the regional park system and offers the visitor a wide range of recreational, environmental, and historical experiences. Tilden was named after Major Charles Lee Tilden, a park founder and the first president of the park district's board of directors. Although hard to imagine, the area, now thick with introduced eucalyptus and Monterey pine, was once a vast grassland with oak-filled valleys.

Largely undeveloped, 2,197-acre Wildcat Regional Park lies adjacent and to the northwest of Tilden. Today, few could guess Wildcat's tumultuous past. Battles over disputed land between Mexican land grant owners, squatters, and speculators occured between 1870 and 1882. From 1882 to 1920, the battles switched to water rights over Wildcat Canyon's once plentiful streams and springs, ending only when East Bay Municipal Utilities District brought water from the Mokelumne River. During the mid-1960s Standard Oil drilled exploratory wells but luckily found too little to exploit. The area was officially named a park in 1976.

Near the intersection of Wildcat Creek Trail and Belgum Trail along the abandoned road and parking area is a sight of additional interest. The cracking and destruction of the road is testament that Wildcat Park straddles the Hayward Fault—reason enough not to encourage building development.

In both Tilden and Wildcat, fox, raccoon, skunk, opposum, deer, and ground squirrel dominate the land while redtail hawk, kestrel, sharp-shinned hawk, Cooper's hawk, and turkey vulture can be seen wheeling over head; if you're out for a sunset ride, you may be lucky enough to see or hear a great horned owl. As you pedal along the canyon, the beauty of the area will go unquestioned. A word of caution—as with most bay area parks, poison oak is prevalent everywhere.

Getting There

Located just north and east of the University of California Berkeley. From Interstate 80, exit at University Avenue and follow University to Martin Luther King. Turn left on Martin Luther King and drive to Marin. Turn right on Marin and continue until Marin runs into Spruce. Turn left on Spruce and drive until you run into an intersection at Spruce Gate with Grizzly, Wildcat Canyon, and Canon drives. Turn left on Canon Drive. Descend on Canon Drive to Central Park Drive and turn right. Drive past the Pony Rides and turn left on Lone Oak Road to the day-use parking area for the playing field and Lone Oak Picnic area. The Loop Trail trailhead is just up Lone Oak Road at the gated entrance.

The Ride

To preserve both the enviroment and your sanity, this ride is best experienced when the trail is relatively dry. We encountered severe mud on one attempt that completely clogged up our bike's derailleurs, forks, chains, you name it, requiring us to hike out carrying our bikes and an additional 40-plus unplanned pounds of mud. It was a unique experience to say the least.

Beginning at the car, ride .2 mile uphill past the Lone Oak Picnic Area to the Raccoon Group Camp and the start of the Loop Trail. Follow the Loop Trail .8 mile to the intersection with Wildcat Creek Trail and Jewel Lake. It is worth stepping off the bikes for a minute here to enjoy the beauty of Jewel Lake. When ready, continue right on the Wildcat Creek Trail to the boundary with Wildcat Regional Park at .9 mile. The dirt road remains relatively flat with a few brief ups and downs for the next 2.3 miles until encountering an abandonded paved road and parking area. Note the impact of the Hayward Fault upon this area. Continue straight .8 rolling mile until the intersection with Belgum Trail. Bear right on Belgum

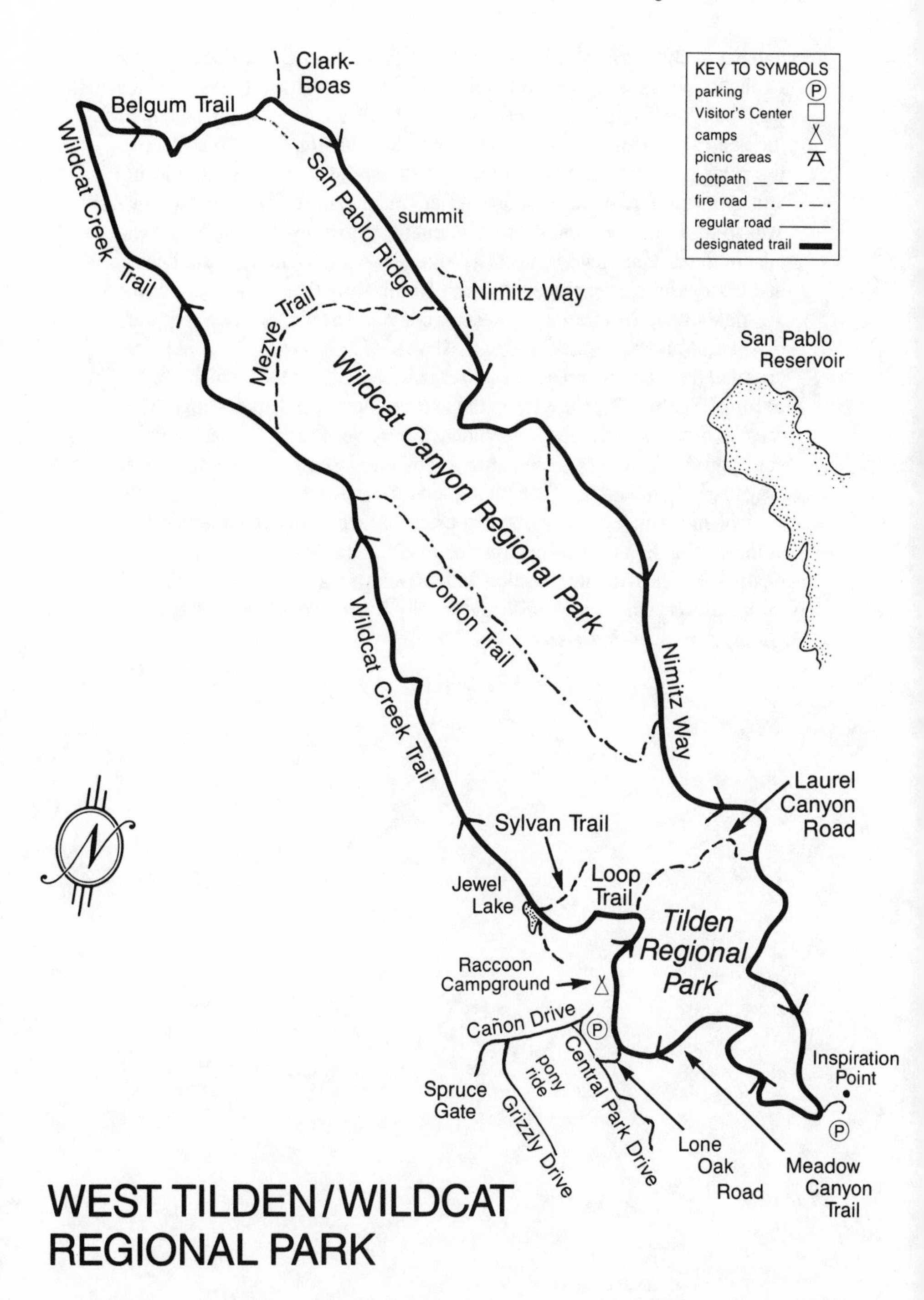
KEY TO SYMBOLS
parking
Visitor's Center
camps
picnic areas
footpath
fire road
regular road
designated trail
Clark-Boas
Belgum Trail
Wildcat Creek Trail
San Pablo Ridge
summit
Nimitz Way
Mezve Trail
Wildcat Canyon Regional Park
San Pablo Reservoir
Conlon Trail
Wildcat Creek Trail
Nimitz Way
Laurel Canyon Road
Sylvan Trail
Loop Trail
Jewel Lake
Tilden Regional Park
Raccoon Campground
Cañon Drive
pony ride
Central Park Drive
Spruce Gate
Grizzly Drive
Lone Oak Road
Meadow Canyon Trail
Inspiration Point
WEST TILDEN / WILDCAT REGIONAL PARK

and begin climbing sharply .9 mile to the junction of Clark Boas and San Pablo Ridge trails. Ignore the unmarked road to the right and continue past the Clark Boas Trail several hundred yards where you will encounter the San Pablo Ridge Trail cutoff to the right. The San Pablo Trail follows the ridgeline over the next 1.3 miles with several very steep uphills and a final downhill past the cutoff to Mezue Trail and the meeting with Nimitz Way .3 mile later. We found an excellent place to enjoy a lunch break and take in the distant views of the Bay, Mount Tamalpais, and Mount Diablo at a high point on the ridge. Once on Nimitz Way there is an option; the 4.2-mile trail to Inspiration Point is paved, gently rolling, and heavily used by hikers, bikers, and equestrians. If you wish to avoid the sometimes crowded (particularly on weekends) conditions, exit on the Conlon Trail—approximately 1.2 miles from the Nimitz and San Pablo Ridge Trail intersection—and descend to Wildcat Creek Trail. Turn left and retrace your path back to the parking area. If you chooose to proceed on Nimitz Way use extra caution; it is easy to pick up excessive speed. Stay in tight control and remember to call out courteously when passing others. Once at Inspiration Point, turn right on Curran Trail and begin descending, now on dirt, .1 mile to the intersection with Meadows Canyon Trail. Head right on Meadows Canyon for a wild and bumpy 1.5-mile descent back to Lone Oak and the parking area.

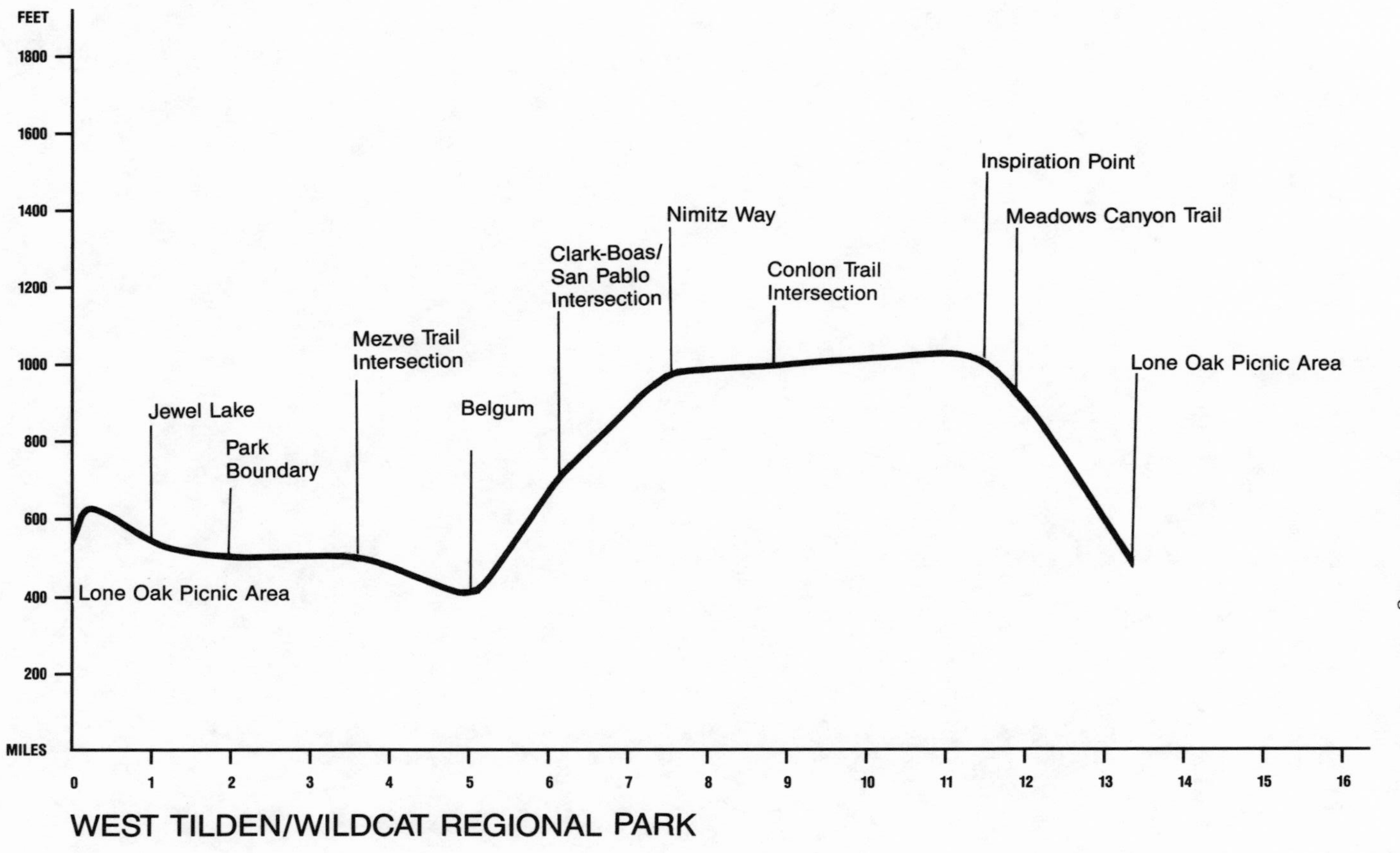
FEET
1800
1600
1400
1200
1000
800
600
400
200
MILES
0
1
2
3
4
5
6
7
8
9
10
11
12
13
14
15
16
Lone Oak Picnic Area
Jewel Lake
Park Boundary
Mezve Trail Intersection
Belgum
Clark-Boas/ San Pablo Intersection
Nimitz Way
Conlon Trail Intersection
Inspiration Point
Meadows Canyon Trail
Lone Oak Picnic Area
WEST TILDEN/WILDCAT REGIONAL PARK

Chapter 11
EAST TILDEN REGIONAL PARK

TRAILHEAD: *Seaview Trail*
TOPO: *Briones Valley*
OVERALL DIFFICULTY: *Easy/Moderate*
TECHNICAL DIFFICULTY: *Easy*
DISTANCE: Approx. *3.7 miles*

Highlights

Tilden Regional Park offers tremendous variety and enjoyment to the visitor. Established in 1936, it is one of the park system's three oldest parks. It was named after Major Charles Lee Tilden, a park founder and the first president of the park district's board of directors. Now dominated by eucalyptus and Montery pine, the hills were once vast grassland, with valleys filled by oak, and streams lushly bounded by willow. It is hard to imagine the land without the eucalyptus and pines, and although a changed landscape, it remains magnificent. Views from the easterly ridges, from Inspiration Point to Vollmer Peak, are spectacular. Several of the promentories in between the two are favorite spots to sit and let gentle breezes chase cares away.

Getting There

Located just north and east of the University of California Berkeley. From Highway 24, east of the Caldecott Tunnel, take the Orinda Village exit on Camino Pablo. Drive through Orinda Village to the intersection with Bear Creek Road to the right and Wildcat Canyon Road to the left. Turn left on Wildcat Canyon Road and drive to Inspiration Point and the parking area. The trailhead for Seaview Trail is approximately 200 yards past Inspiration Point and on the left side of Wildcat Canyon Road.

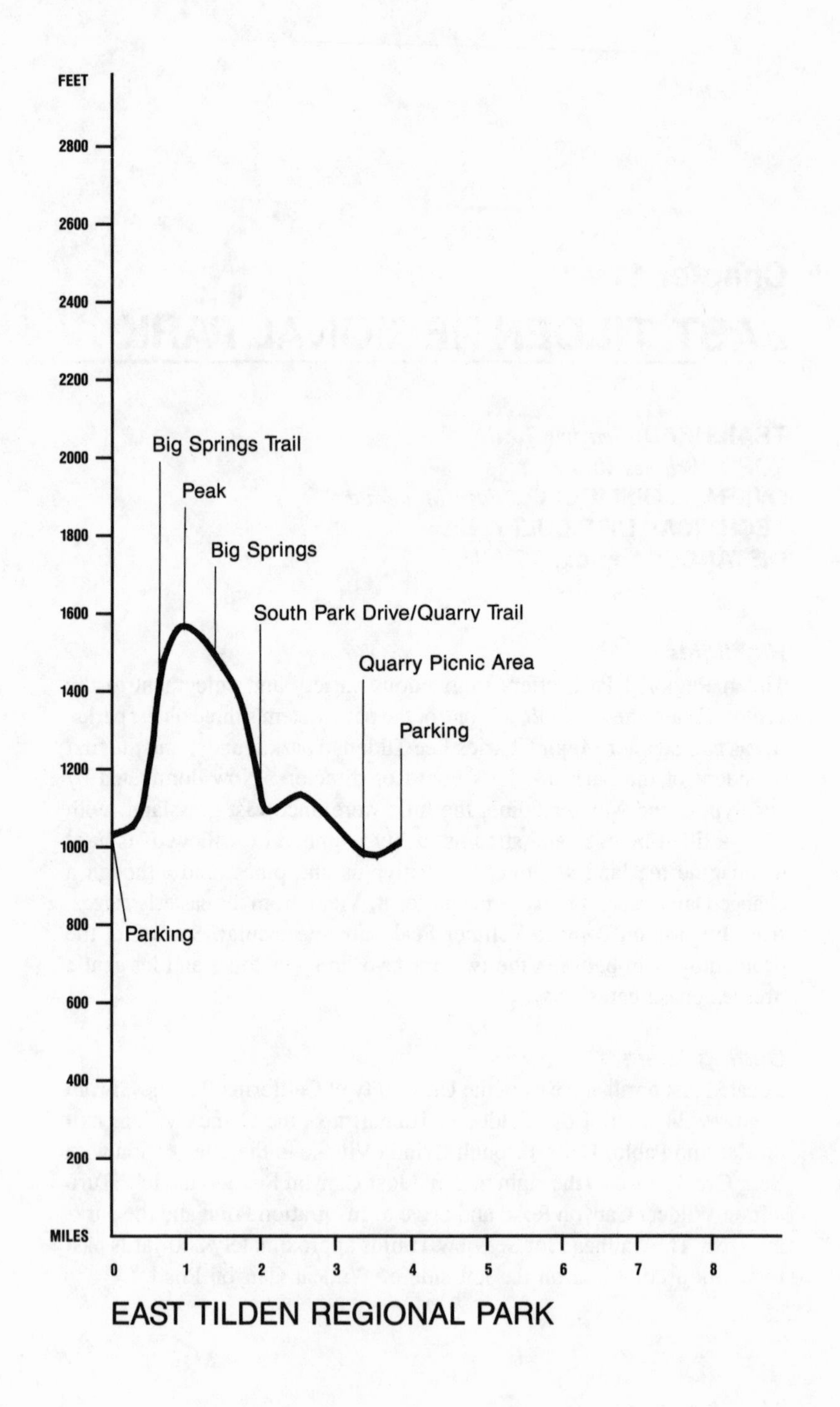

EAST TILDEN REGIONAL PARK

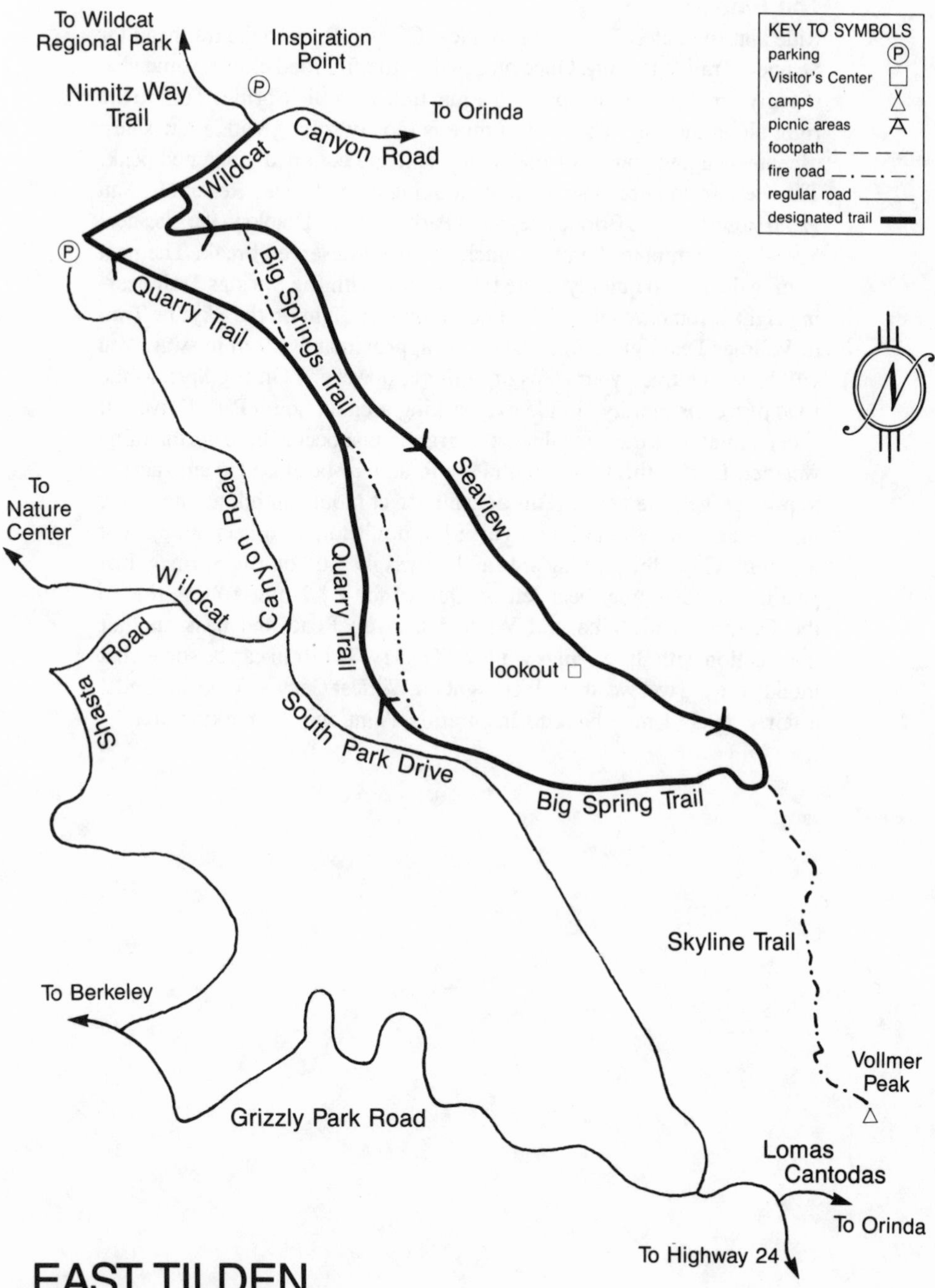

EAST TILDEN
REGIONAL PARK

The Ride

Ride approximately 2 miles on Wildcat Canyon Road to the trailhead for Seaview Trail to the left. Once on Seaview the fire road climbs somewhat sharply for about .5 mile passing a junction with Big Springs Trail to the right along the way. The next .5 mile is mostly rolling with a few sharp ascents bringing you to a wonderful picnic table atop an unnamed peak. The view from here is spectacular looking over Briones Reservoir, San Pablo Reservoir, the Briones Regional Park, and Mt. Diablo in the distance. Spend a few minutes here for lunch or a well-deserved break. The next .3 mile drops you quickly to the intersection with Big Springs Trail bearing right. (You have an option of continuing straight on the Skyline Trail to Vollmer Peak, elevation 1,913 feet, approximately .9 mile away. You will have to retrace your steps once there, however.) On Big Springs the road descends rapidly .6 mile to a parking area on South Park Drive. Of special interest is the annual newt migration that occurs here during rainy weather. During this time, South Park Road may be closed to auto access to protect the little newts. This doesn't affect mountain biking, however, just the auto access via South Park; but don't forget to keep an eye out for them. Cross the parking area and bear right, still on Big Springs. Just past the parking area, bear left on Quarry for a 1.2-mile rolling ride to the Quarry Picnic area and Wildcat Canyon Road and pass another intersection with Big Springs while on Quarry. This trail can be somewhat muddy during wet weather. Turn right on Wildcat Canyon Road and pedal a fairly level .4 mile back to Inspiration Point and the parking area.

Chapter Twelve

REDWOOD REGIONAL PRESERVE

TRAILHEAD: *Canyon Trail, Canyon Meadow Staging Area*
TOPO: *Oakland East*
OVERALL DIFFICULTY: *Moderate/Strenuous*
TECHNICAL DIFFICULTY: *Moderate*
DISTANCE: *8.5 miles*

Highlights

Redwood Regional Park is a peaceful escape from the nearby noise and congestion of downtown Oakland. It is also an area with the unique distinction of being the location where rainbow trout were first identified as a distinct species. The protected trout still spawn in Redwood Creek after migrating from a downstream reservoir outside of the park; fishing is prohibited. Redwood Regional Park is perhaps best known for its magnificent stands of 150-foot-plus coast redwoods, the *Sequoia sempervirens*. In 1826 the ship logs of the Royal Navy indicated several of the huge redwoods to be used as navigational landmarks from sightings made 16 miles from what is now Golden Gate. While much of the park was heavily logged in the mid-1800s, the second-growth stand of redwoods remains impressive. The 1,830-acre park also includes evergreen, chaparral, and open grasslands. If you start your ride early enough in the morning, before the throngs begin hitting the trail, you will stand a good chance of seeing deer, raccoon, and perhaps the rare golden eagle hunting rabbit or squirrel. There are several group camping areas available within the park; call 415-531-9043 for more information.

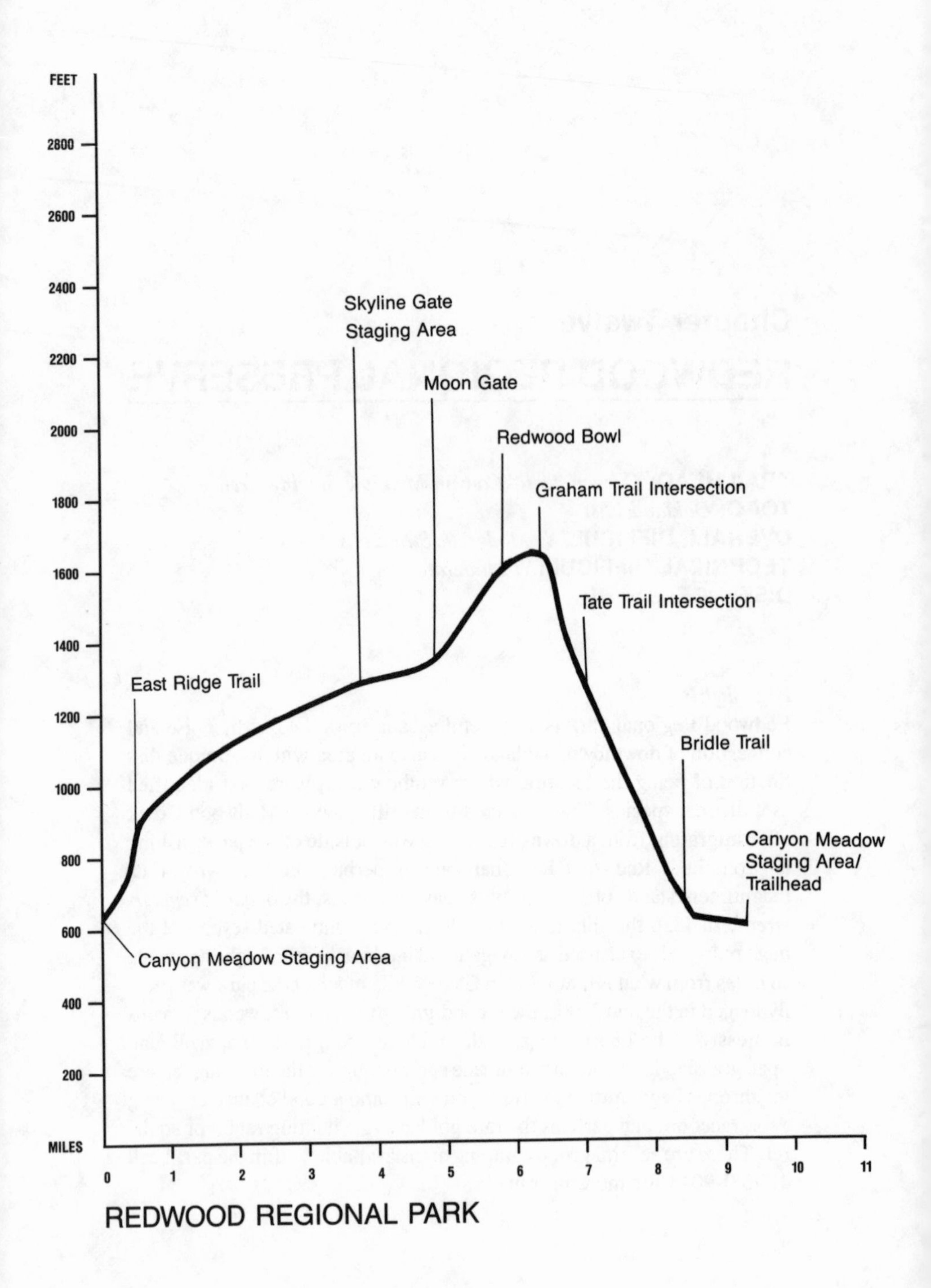

REDWOOD REGIONAL PARK

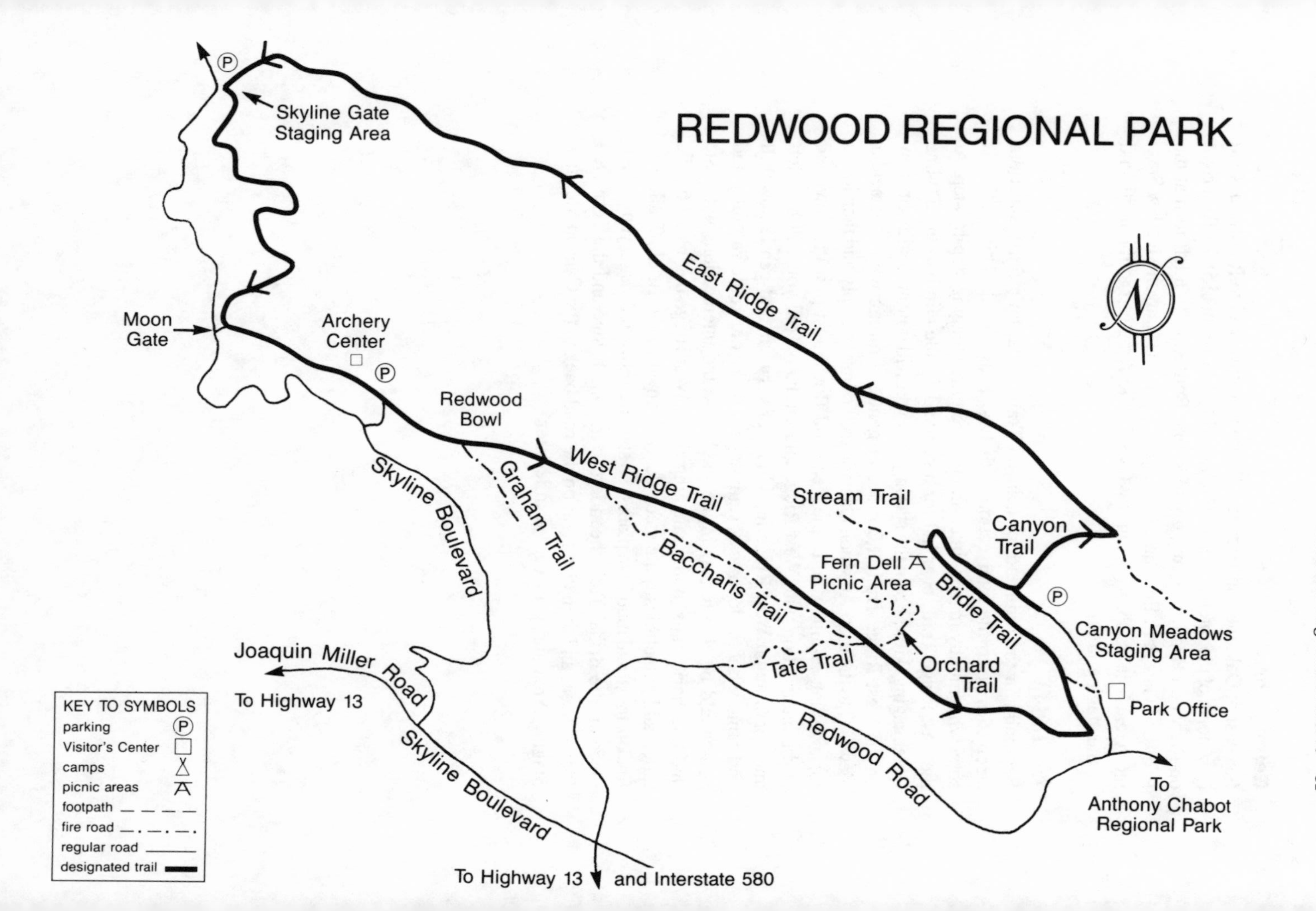
REDWOOD REGIONAL PARK
Skyline Gate Staging Area
Moon Gate
Archery Center
Redwood Bowl
East Ridge Trail
West Ridge Trail
Graham Trail
Skyline Boulevard
Stream Trail
Canyon Trail
Fern Dell Picnic Area
Bridle Trail
Baccharis Trail
Tate Trail
Orchard Trail
Canyon Meadows Staging Area
Park Office
Redwood Road
To Anthony Chabot Regional Park
Joaquin Miller Road
To Highway 13
Skyline Boulevard
To Highway 13 and Interstate 580
KEY TO SYMBOLS
parking
Visitor's Center
camps
picnic areas
footpath
fire road
regular road
designated trail

Getting There

Just east of Oakland and Highway 13. Take Highway 13 to Redwood Road (just north of the intersection of Highway 13 and Interstate 580.) Turn right on Redwood Road, crossing over Skyline Boulevard to a left turn at the Redwood Gate Park Entrance. Leave your car at the Canyon Meadow Staging Area. The trailhead begins by Owl Picnic Area just to the north end of the staging area.

The Ride

Beginning at the trailhead for Canyon Trail, pedal up a fairly short but steep .5 mile to the intersection with East Ridge Trail. This section is somewhat muddy in the winter and may require slogging step-by-step. At the East Ridge Trail, bear left for a gentle 3.3-mile climb to the Skyline Gate Staging Area. From the staging area you will continue straight, now on the West Ridge Trail, 1.2 miles of gentle climbing with spectacular views off to the east. At Moon Gate the trail climbs sharply and then levels for a rolling .8-mile ride to the Redwood Bowl. Just past the Bowl and at the intersection with West Ridge and Graham Trail you will bear left and continue on West Ridge for 1 mile of very fun and gentle downhill and rapid whooptydoo rocky stair steps—pick your route carefully and you should be able to stay in the saddle. At the intersections with Tate and Baccharis trails, both branching right, West Ridge begins a 1.6-mile quick and sometimes quite steep descent down to the Bridle Trail. The track is loose and muddy in places, so stay in control and watch your speed. Once on the Bridal Trail, head left to a stone bridge and the Fern Dell Picnic Area, and then turn right on the road back to the Canyon Meadow Staging Area and your car, .8 mile later.

Chapter Thirteen

ANTHONY CHABOT REGIONAL PARK

TRAILHEAD: *Chabot City Park/West Shore Trail*
TOPO: *Oakland East, Las Trampas Ridge, Hayward*
OVERALL DIFFICULTY: *Moderate*
TECHNICAL DIFFICULTY: *Easy*
DISTANCE: *Approximately 13.6 miles*

Highlights

Probably best known for its fishing and boating, Anthony Chabot is an excellent park for hiking, biking, and equestrian use. It is also well known for Chabot Family Camp, with tent, trailer, and walk-in campsites. The camp has hot showers and is a first-class base for exploring the park and surrounding environment. Call 415-531-9043 for more information.

Chabot Regional Park is a 4,927-acre preserve named after Anthony Chabot, the California businessman who created Lake Chabot by building an earthen dam. Originally frequented by Indians for food gathering, the lands were later used for cattle ranching. In the early 1900s the region was converted into watershed lands for the city of Oakland by the People's Water Company. The water company later became the East Bay Municipal Utility District in 1928 and now leases the lake to the park for public use.

While the area around the lake itself is quite crowded, especially on weekends, the inland trails away from the lake offer miles of excellent biking through grasslands, chaparral, and shady eucalyptus groves. The East Bay Skyline National Trail, crossing over 31 miles of East Bay land from Richmond to Castro Valley, runs the length of Anthony Chabot and is open to mountain bikes while in the park.

Getting There

Located just east of Interstate 580 and Oakland International Airport. Take the Fairmont Drive exit and follow Fairmont Drive to a left turn on Lake Chabot Road (to the right is the parking for Lake Chabot Marina). Turn right on Estudillo Avenue and head over the narrow bridge into the parking area for the City of San Leandro Chabot Park. The trailhead is beyond the gate at the far end of the parking area.

The Ride

Beginning at the parking area, ride through the gate and up .6 mile on a paved fire road to the intersection with Bass Cove Trail and West Shore Trail. Bear right on West Shore Trail for 1.8 miles of rolling and paved road to the Lake Chabot Marina. Use extreme caution through here as there are lots of hikers, bikers, and fishermen using the trail. At the Marina bear left on the East Shore Trail and ride 1.4 rolling miles to the intersection with Cameron Loop and the end of the paved trail. Pedal another .2 mile to the second junction with Cameron Loop heading right and proceed across a narrow bridge to the left. Once over the bridge, bear right up the Live Oak Trail 1.2 miles to the junction with the Towhee Trail on the right and a road heading left to the Anthony Chabot Family Campground. Continue right and up the Towhee Trail to the top of the ridge and the intersection of Brandon and Redtail trails. Turn left onto the Redtail Trail and continue past a day-use parking area, the Marksmanship Range, and another intersection with the Brandon Trail bearing left; continue past the Marciel Staging Area and descend to the intersection with the Grass Valley Trail—total mileage on the Redtail, 2.1 miles. At the Grass Valley Trail we recommend taking time for a picnic lunch on one of the grassy spots near the stream. When ready, pedal 1 mile along the relatively flat Grass Valley Trail through several cattle gates and to the Bort Meadow Staging Area. Head left and now back up the other side of the valley on the Brandon Trail.

(If you wish a very long ride it is possible to continue straight 2.3 miles on the East Bay Skyline Trail instead of turning left on the Brandon Trail. This will connect you with Redwood Regional Park and Redwood Road. Bear right on Redwood Road and pedal to the park office and the Canyon Meadow Staging Area, where you can join our described Redwood Park ride at the Canyon Trail. The Redwood Loop is approximately 8.3 miles, so this would make for quite a long but enjoyable day—be prepared and start early.)

Continue pedaling 1.8 miles past the cutoff to the equestrian center and the stone bridge and up the Jackson Grade to the intersection with Goldenrod Trail and a day-use parking area on Skyline Boulevard. Head

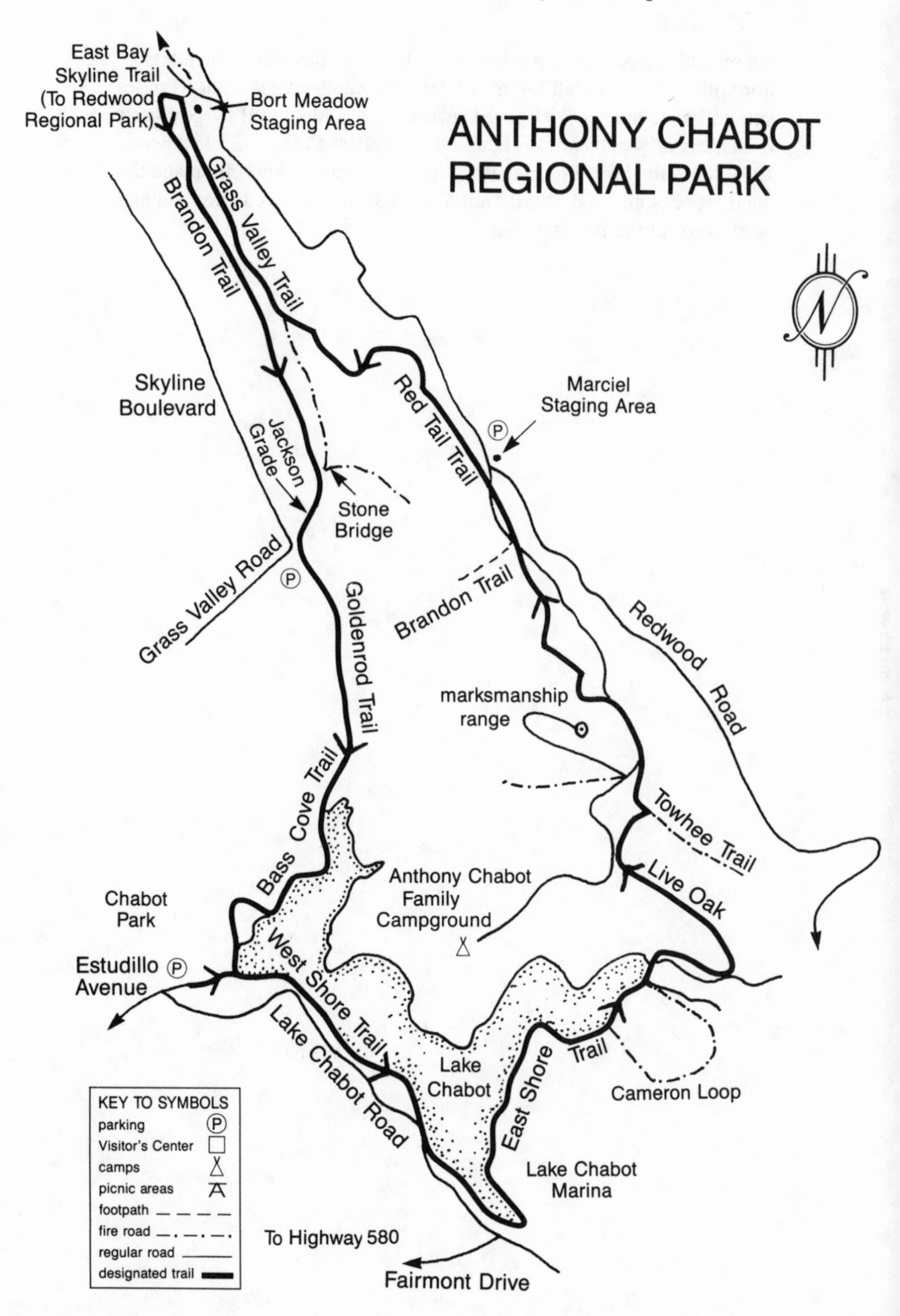

ANTHONY CHABOT
REGIONAL PARK
East Bay
Skyline Trail
(To Redwood
Regional Park)
Bort Meadow
Staging Area
Grass Valley Trail
Brandon Trail
Skyline
Boulevard
Jackson
Grade
Stone
Bridge
Red Tail Trail
Marciel
Staging Area
Grass Valley Road
Goldenrod Trail
Brandon Trail
Redwood
Road
marksmanship
range
Bass Cove Trail
Towhee Trail
Live Oak
Anthony Chabot
Family
Campground
Chabot
Park
Estudillo
Avenue
West Shore Trail
Lake Chabot Road
Lake
Chabot
East Shore
Trail
Cameron Loop
Lake Chabot
Marina
To Highway 580
Fairmont Drive
KEY TO SYMBOLS
parking
Visitor's Center
camps
picnic areas
footpath
fire road
regular road
designated trail

left on Goldenrod Trail a gradual, though steady, descent to the intersection with Bass Cove Trail 1.4 miles later. (Use caution because at 1.1 miles you will encounter a brief paved section that is also used by golf carts from the nearby golf course.) Bear left on the Bass Cove Trail and descend 1.1 miles to the lake. Proceed along its banks until a short climb and the intersection with West Shore Trail. Turn left on the paved fire road and head down to the parking area.

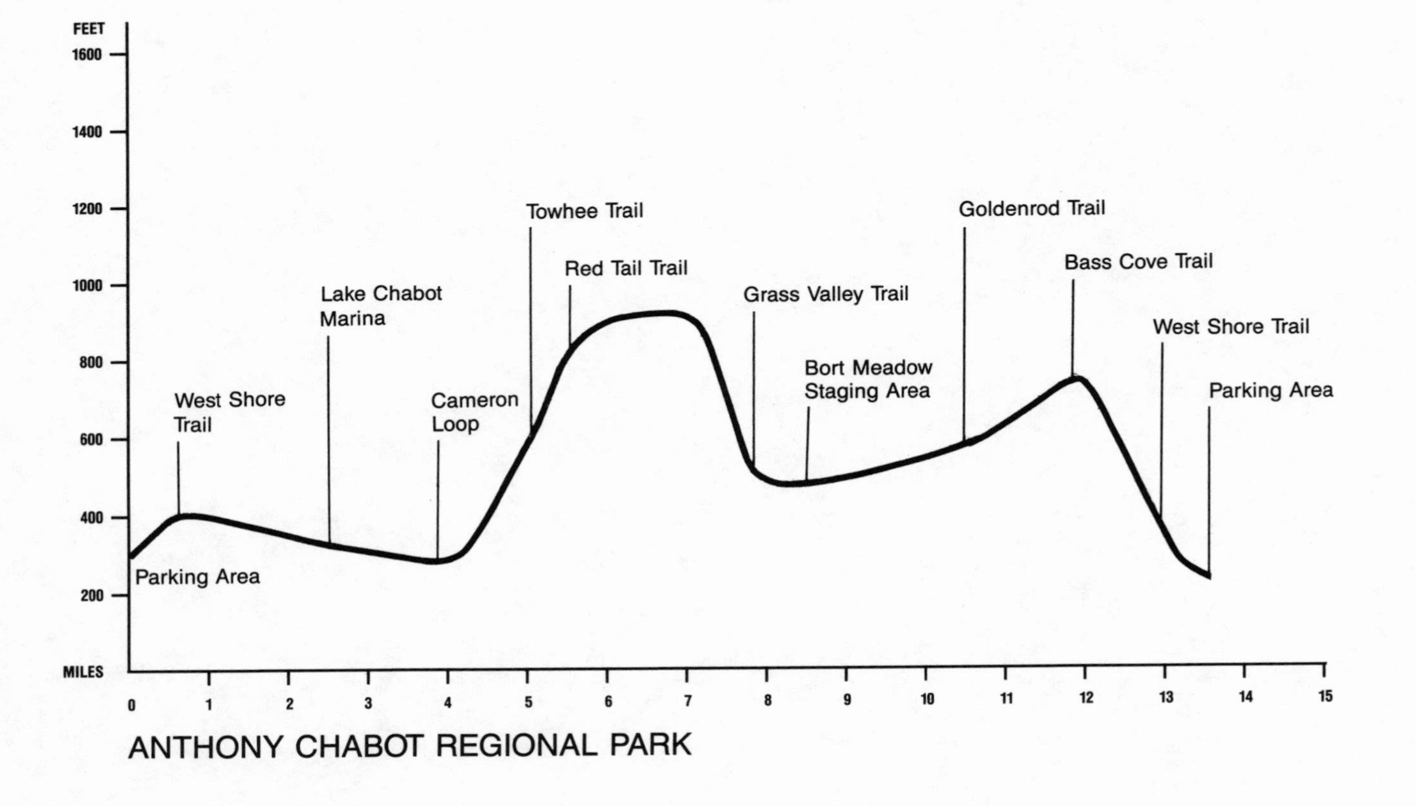
FEET
1600
1400
1200
1000
800
600
400
200
MILES
0
1
2
3
4
5
6
7
8
9
10
11
12
13
14
15
Parking Area
West Shore Trail
Lake Chabot Marina
Cameron Loop
Towhee Trail
Red Tail Trail
Grass Valley Trail
Bort Meadow Staging Area
Goldenrod Trail
Bass Cove Trail
West Shore Trail
Parking Area
ANTHONY CHABOT REGIONAL PARK

Cycling Necessities

TIRE IRONS
PATCH KIT
SPARE TUBE
TIRE PUMP
CHAIN TOOL
APPROPRIATE SELECTION OF TIRE WRENCHES: check with bike shop
SPOKE WRENCH
SPARE SPOKES: (for your wheel type) these can be taped to the chain stay
CHANGE FOR A PHONE CALL
FIRST AID KIT: assorted bandaids, ace bandage, 3x3 gauze pads, adhesive tape, moleskin, aspirin, antiseptic, tincture of Benzoin, needle, matches, sunscreen, water purification tablets
WATER BOTTLE: Your body needs a minimum of 2 quarts of fluid per day, so plan accordingly!
COMPASS
SMALL LIGHT: flashlight, headlamp, or bike light
HIGH-ENERGY MUNCHIES: gorp, nuts, cheese, dried fruit.

For an overnight add the following items to the above list:
MOUNTAIN BIKE REAR PANNIER RACK: even if you are opting not to use panniers, the rack gives you a surface to which you can attach a tent and sleeping bag and also minimizes the inevitable brown racing stripe on your back in wet and muddy terrain
SMALL BIKE PANNIERS AND/OR LARGE FANNY PACK: use whatever system maintains optimum agility and balance
SMALL STOVE AND FUEL
COMPACT COOK POT, 1 TO 2 QUARTS
COMPACT AND LIGHTWEIGHT DOWN SLEEPING BAG

COMPACT AND LIGHTWEIGHT TENT/BIVI SACK
SMALL KNIFE
SMALL SPOON
WATERPROOF/WINDPROOF MATCHES

The Well-Dressed Rider

With the exception of shorts and helmet, riding attire can be adequately improvised with clothing that you may already own. Following is a list that will span the broad range of temperatures that can occur in the Bay Area. As with all active sports, layers must be thin and lightweight to allow for exact temperature adjustments; no single layer should be exceptionally warm. With the exception of t-shirts and socks, it is best to avoid cotton, which dries slowly.

HELMET: An absolute necessity. Spend as much as you can possibly afford (how much is your head worth?); this is not a place to try and save some money! We recommend a helmet with some sort of shell on the exterior; this will help protect your head from sharp objects and extend the helmet's life.

SHORTS: Specialized cycling shorts are well worth the money. After spending several hours in the saddle those seemingly innocent seams on the butt of your walking shorts can feel like mountainous ridges. We recommend lycra or wool with a chamois or synthetic crotch pad.

SHOES: These should be stiff-soled and provide good traction when walking becomes a necessity. Specific mountain biking boots are nice, but hiking footwear, low- or high-top can be substituted with good results; check to be sure they are easy to operate with toe clips.

GLOVES: Make sure they have dense padding in the palms. Lightweight cross-country ski gloves work great for early mornings or cold days.

SHIRT: Cycling jerseys with backpockets are nice, but a cotton t-shirt works just fine. Avoid lycra—it's clammy!

SUNGLASSES: These do much more than go along for the ride to make you look cool! They provide eye protection from bugs, wind, and dust, in addition to ultraviolet rays. Plastic (polycarbonate) lenses are lightweight and the best for safety, although they scratch easily. Specific sport or cycling glasses provide the most comfort and protection, despite giving the wearer a slightly alien appearance.

RAIN JACKET/WINDBREAKER: The choices here are numerous. Waterproof, nonbreathable materials should be avoided since they tend to make it feel like there's a rainstorm of perspiration inside your jacket. Some opt for cape-like rainwear, but we've found these tend to act like a sail when there are windy conditions. Specifically designed cycling jackets work great, are well-ventilated and are cut longer in the back to prevent that chilly gap of bare skin. Lightweight rain jackets made of Gore-Tex or other types of waterproof/breathable materials designed for backpacking or hiking are also fine.

LONG UNDERWEAR TOP: For cooler weather. Synthetic is recommended. Long-sleeve cycling jerseys are also nice, though not essential. Avoid cotton.

TIGHTS/LONG UNDERWEAR BOTTOMS: For cold weather. Also must be synthetic. Lycra cross-country ski tights work well.

This is not an all-inclusive listing. Add or delete items depending on the weather and your personal needs.

Rider's Responsibility

At the time of publication, all of the rides described within these pages were legal. However, because of political pressures, environmental damage, and other mitigating circumstances, any trail may be closed at any time. Please, plan your trip carefully and call ahead to the appropriate agency to determine legality of trails and conditions of their use. Even if described in this book, do not ride on a trail that has been closed to use.

EAST BAY REGIONAL PARK DISTRICT
11500 Skyline Blvd.
Oakland, CA 94619
415-531-9300

MOUNT DIABLO STATE PARK
P.O. Box 250
Diablo, CA 94528
415-837-2525

SUGARLOAF STATE PARK
2605 Adobe Canyon Rd.
Kenwood, CA 95452
707-833-5712

ANNADEL STATE PARK
6201 Channel Drive
Santa Rosa, CA 95409
707-539-3911

GOLDEN GATE NATIONAL RECREATION AREA
Marin Headquarters
Fort Cronkhite, CA 94965
415-331-1540

MOUNT TAMALPAIS STATE PARK
Pantoll Ranger Station
801 Panoramic Highway
Mill Valley, CA 94941
415-399-2070

MARIN MUNICIPAL WATER DISTRICT
220 Nellen Ave.
Corte Madera, CA 94925
415-924-4600

POINT REYES NATIONAL SEA SHORE
Point Reyes, CA 94956
415-663-1092

SAMUEL P. TAYLOR STATE PARK
P.O. Box 251
Lagunitas, CA 94938
415-488-9897

Bike Clubs and Trail Organizations

The following is a list of various bicycle clubs and organizations in the Bay Area that work actively to promote responsible land use and access. Through support and active participation, you can help ensure trail preservation and present a unified and responsible image of mountain biking to all.

BICYCLE TRAILS COUNCIL OF THE EAST BAY
P.O. Box 9583
Berkeley, CA 94709
415-527-6617

BICYCLE TRAILS COUNCIL OF MARIN
P.O. Box 13842
San Rafael, CA 94913
415-479-5482

RESPONSIBLE ORGANIZED MOUNTAIN PEDALERS
218 Victor Ave.
Campbell, CA 95008
408-866-1744

TRAIL CENTER
4898 El Camino Real, #205A
Los Altos, CA 94022
415-968-7065

INTERNATIONAL MOUNTAIN BICYCLE ASSOCIATION
Route 2, Box 303
Bishop, CA 93514
619-387-2412

The Green Belt Of Sanity

We are fortunate to be able to live in a city surrounded by a relative green belt of sanity—a collection of parks and preserves dedicated to restoring the mind. These have not occurred accidentally, but have been the product of much hard work, both within the courtroom and on the trail. It seems that some feel undeveloped land is in need of being "improved" by man, be it by bulldozer or trail crew. Imagine the Bay Area without regional or state parks—lands that, instead of being open for all of our enjoyment, were tied up as private holdings for the profit and exploit of a privileged few.

There is still much open space that is in danger of being sacrificed for development in the form of shopping malls or industrial complexes. Without your help these places may be lost, never to be enjoyed by our children. Imagine if those who came before us never fought to ensure future enjoyment and public access to such beautiful locations as Pt. Reyes, Mt. Diablo, or Wildcat Canyon. Following is a list of organizations, both grass roots and national that need your help in the form of money, volunteer time, or even a few moments spent writing a card to senators or congressmen. Please help to ensure that others will also be able to enjoy our green belt.

GREEN BELT ALLIANCE
116 New Montgomery, Suite 640
San Francisco, CA 94105
415-543-4291

TRUST FOR PUBLIC LAND
116 New Montgomery
San Francisco, CA 94105
415-495-4014

RESTORING THE EARTH
1713 C Martin Luther King Jr. Blvd.
Berkeley, CA 94709
415-843-2645

NATURE CONSERVANCY
785 Market Street, 3rd Floor
San Francisco, CA 94103
415-777-0487

ABOUT THE AUTHORS

MICHAEL HODGSON is a free-lance writer and author living in the Bay Area. The wilderness has been part of his life since early childhood. An experienced cross-country ski instructor, mountaineer, and mountain biker, Michael most enjoys sharing his love for the outdoors, through his writing.

MARK LORD's interests span backcountry ski mountaineering and climbing, ocean kayaking, long-distance cycle touring, and mountain biking. Mark, a resident of the Santa Cruz mountains, has also authored a guide to ski touring at Lake Tahoe and is a free-lance writer and guide.